four boys
in the
White House

**the children of
James and Ellen White**

First published 2008
Copyright © 2008

British Library Cataloguing in Publication Data.
A catalogue record for this book is available
from the British Library.

ISBN 978-1-904685-50-0

Published by The Stanborough Press,
Grantham, Lincolnshire.

Printed in Thailand.

four boys
in the
White House

the children of
James and Ellen White

by
Paul B. Ricchiuti

Dedication

This book is dedicated to the loving memory of my sister Marianne LaBute. In later life she liked to spell her first name in two parts, Mary Ann. I like the way she used to spell it, Marianne. In her long, hard years of fighting cancer, her attitude was always positive. She never once lost her sense of humour, and she loved the Lord more than her own life. She was a devoted wife and mother, and I was, and am proud to be, her brother. She was one of the bravest persons I have ever known. I shall always love her, and I know that God will, too.

Photographs courtesy of The Ellen G. White Estate, Inc.

Table of Contents

The White Home: Some Background Details

Ellen (1827-1915) and James (1821-1881) were co-founders of the Seventh-day Adventist Church. Ellen (Harmon) was born in a farm home near the village of Gorham, Maine, of sturdy New England stock.

James was born in Palmyra, Maine, his father being descended from one of 'the Pilgrim Fathers' who arrived in 1620 on the ship *Mayflower.*

Both Ellen and James were caught up in the revival led by William Miller. They were married by the Justice of the Peace in Portland, Maine, on 30 August 1846. For the first year of their married life James and Ellen lived with Ellen's parents at Portland, then at Gorham, Maine. Ellen had had her first vision in December 1844, aged 17. Her courtship of James had begun by then and, in subsequent months, they sought to build courage into the remnants of Miller's movement following the Great Disappointment while, at the same time, combating fanaticism.

During the years in which the Whites emerged as leaders of the developing Advent movement they became parents. Their first child, Henry Nichols, was born on 26 August 1847 and their second, James Edson, was born – in Rocky Hill, Connecticut – in July 1849.

By that time both James and Ellen were involved in an exacting preaching, writing and publishing ministry. They travelled a great deal and each was absent from home (and one another) for significant periods.

Money was in short supply. They moved, first, to Rochester, New York, then, to Battle Creek, Michigan. The pressures on the White family were immense and the discouragements considerable. In August 1854 their third son, William Clarence, was born.

After the move to Michigan both Whites carried prodigious workloads occasioned by the establishment of a publishing ministry and the development of church organisation. There were long journeys by wagon, by train and by sleigh. These long journeys, often through sparsely settled country, brought many adventures. There were stories of remarkable providences. They experienced both victories and setbacks as they spearheaded the main evangelistic thrust of the Advent movement.

The last of their four sons, John Herbert, was born on 20 September 1860. By then the White family numbered two parents and four boys, the eldest of whom was 13. But the family circle was not to remain unbroken for long.

How did Ellen and James manage as parents? What were the stories of the four boys born into the White house?

Editor

Introduction

The world of the 1800s and early 1900s was filled with mystery, hardship, adventure, excitement, and, once in a while, fun. Let's take a look.

The United States was a wild and half-wild stretch of hills, mountains and valleys, covering 3,000 miles of seemingly endless land in all directions. In its centre were thousands of acres of empty plains. They were called the Great American Desert. Yet they were not entirely empty. There were Indians, and great furry beasts called buffalo grazed on most of those plains.

In Europe, royal families continued to wear glittering crowns and hold great banquets in their massive castles and palaces. They hardly noticed the unnumbered poor as they laid down their hoes and rakes, packed the few belongings they owned and then crossed the frightening Atlantic Ocean. They had gone to America and an island in New York harbour named Ellis. There were twelve million of them between the years 1892 and 1954. With tears in their eyes they slowly passed the giant 305-feet-tall Statue of Liberty and knew they had found home in a new land. My father was one of them.

But that was not all. Gold was discovered in 1849 in California, and following that, a whole nation sang *Old Susanna.*

Then the way was opened for new cities and little puffing engines pulling passenger cars. Those were trains that had their beginnings at Promontory Point in Utah. The year was 1869. A solid gold spike was the last thing driven into a wooden tie.

I remember standing before the thick glass window of a heavy black safe at the Stanford University Museum in

California, and looking longingly at that spike. It's still there today.

With the coming of the railroad, the Pony Express vanished, and towns and cities such as Dodge City and Abilene sprang to life. Travel across the country was reduced from months to just six days! That gave rise to well-known personalities such as Billy the Kid, Wyatt Earp, Calamity Jane, Wild Bill Hickok and Buffalo Bill. They were all westerners.

In the eastern section of the nation arose other famous names, such as Abraham Lincoln, Sojourner Truth, Jenny Lind, Teddy Roosevelt, Diamond Jim Brady and Annie Oakley. And who can forget Mark Twain and the whitewashed fences in *The Adventures of Tom Sawyer?*

It was a fast-moving time in the history of humankind. Inventions were exploding on the scene, such as the telegraph in 1844, the typewriter in 1868, the telephone in 1878, and Edison's light bulb in 1879. Horseless carriages called automobiles began to move, and movie cameras rolled.

New York City increased its population from 3,000 in 1810 to over 100,000 in 1850. Twenty years later, following the horrors of the American Civil War, with its dramatic Underground Railroad, the Brooklyn Bridge was opened. The year was 1870.

Into that changing world were born four small boys who lived in the White house, the home of James and Ellen G. White. Let's look inside and find out what it was like.

Bibliography

This Fabulous Century, 1870, prelude 1900, published by Time-Life Books, copyright 1970.
Kids Discover, 149 Fifth Avenue, New York, NY, 10010.

John Herbert

John Herbert was born in Battle Creek, Michigan, on Thursday 20 September 1860. It is thought the Whites were hoping for a girl and this may be one reason why the baby went without a name for almost three months. Another reason for the absence of a name could be the mother's protracted return to health and strength after delivering the baby. James remained with her for three weeks after the birth; then he went away to conference meetings in Iowa and Wisconsin.

But there were letters between the two while he travelled and he was worried about his wife's health. In one note she said she was doing well but that she was staying in bed in the parlour and planned to continue to do so for another week. Then she added she was 'still a cripple.'[1]

Mrs White also said, 'You may be assured I miss your little visits in my room, but the thought you are doing the will of God helps me bear the loss of your company.'[2]

It is from the letters which flowed between them like water that we learn about the new baby.

She wrote, 'Our nameless little one grows finely, weighed him last Wednesday. He then weighed ten pounds and one quarter. He is well.' She ended that letter by saying, 'My hand trembles so, fear you cannot read it. In much love, your Ellen.'[3]

On 22 October 1860 she reported, 'The little nameless one is fat and rugged, and very quiet. Has not had a cold yet.'[4] She finished that letter two days later by adding, 'I must send this today. I am getting along as fast as can be expected. Have had no pullbacks yet. Come up very slowly. The babe is five weeks old tomorrow, a fat, hearty fellow. He takes much nursing. I am very hungry most of the time, appetite good. The children are well.' Then, thinking of the baby again, she added, 'We have just weighed the yet nameless one. He weighs twelve pounds and a half, good weight.'[5]

James wrote a letter that same day, expressing his deep concern for her health. He wrote, 'Be careful of your health. Do not want for anything that money will buy. Remember me affectionately to Henry, Edson, Willie and _____ without a name. Tell them that father prays for them, and loves them very much.'[6]

On 1 November, as James travelled on the Mississippi riverboat *War Eagle*, he wrote, 'I am happy to have you give so good a report of home, of our dear boys. I love my family and nothing but a sense of duty can separate me from them.'[7]

On 2 November, in a letter to a friend named Lucinda Hall, Ellen White told about her condition. She wrote about her weakness and going upstairs on her knees. She also asked Lucinda to think of a name for the baby.

The Whites' other boys, Henry and Edson, also wrote to their father. James answered by writing that he was 'Exceedingly glad to get Henry's and Edson's letters. Good boys! I shall soon be home with them. Kiss Willie and nameless for me.'[8]

In her letter of 19 November Ellen White wrote, 'We are as well as usual. Babe is fat and healthy, weighed last Thursday fifteen pounds. He promises to be a very rugged boy. Babe is quiet and good nights, but I will tell you one thing, he is so healthy it will cost you quite a bill to keep me and him. He eats and throws it up and is just as greedy to eat again. My appetite is good. Food sets well.'[9]

Soon after that letter James had a strong feeling that something was wrong at home. While praying he had an impression that the baby was sick. He pictured him with a dreadfully swollen head and wrote to his wife about it, but three days later, she wrote back saying there was no truth to it.

However, on the following day, the baby was taken seriously ill with erysipelas in the face and head. (This disease, also known as St Anthony's Fire, is a condition to which infants are very susceptible. It is highly infectious and is caused by a specific streptococcus of the skin or mucous membranes.) A telegram was sent to James, and in two days he was home.

Apparently, the family had taken a train ride to visit friends in the country. They were all feeling well, even Mrs White. 'The boys,' she said, 'had a good, free time in the country. I let them run and race as much as they pleased.'[10] But the trip proved deadly for the baby because he contracted erysipelas. Fortunately, Mrs White and the other boys were not affected.

She describes what took place. 'My dear babe was a great sufferer. Twenty-four days and nights we anxiously watched over him, using all the remedies we could for his recovery and earnestly presenting his case to the Lord. At times I could not control my feelings as I witnessed his sufferings. Much of my time was spent in tears, and humble supplications to God.'[11]

It was during this time that the baby was given a name – John Herbert White. On Friday 14 December, Ellen White wrote, 'My babe was worse. I listened to his laboured breathing, and felt his pulseless wrist. I knew that he must die. That was an hour of anguish for me. The icy hand of death was already upon him. We watched his feeble, gasping breath, until it ceased, and we felt thankful that his sufferings were ended.

'When my child was dying, I could not weep. I fainted at the funeral. My heart ached as though it would break, yet I could not shed a tear. . . . We followed our child to Oak Hill Cemetery, there to rest until the Life-giver shall come, and break the fetters of the tomb, and call him forth immortal.

'After we returned from the funeral, my home

seemed lonely. I felt reconciled to the will of God, yet despondency and gloom settled upon me.'[12]

Thus ended the brief life of John Herbert.

References

[1] Arthur L. White, *Ellen G. White, The Early Years,* volume one (The Review and Herald Publishing Association), page 425.

[2-4] *Ibid,* page 426.

[5] *Ibid,* pages 426-7.

[6-7] *Ibid,* page 427.

[8] *Ibid,* page 428.

[9] *Ibid,* page 429.

[10-11] *Ibid,* page 430.

[12] *Ibid,* page 431.

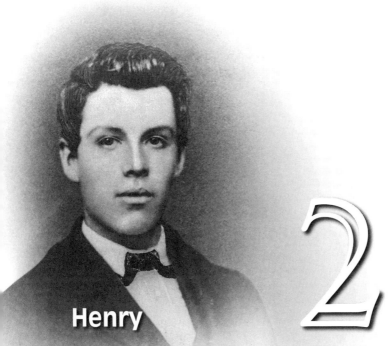

Henry

Henry was the oldest of the four boys in the White house. He had a keen mind and a charming personality. He was handsome, an athlete with a strong build, a musician and a born leader. Above all, Henry was a devoted Christian. From all indications he was sure to be successful in the days ahead and his parents had high hopes for his future.

Henry Nichols White was born in Gorham, Maine, on 26 August 1847. Four months later, Henry was seriously ill. His tiny body was overheated and in pain and swelling settled in his lungs. He grew worse daily and hope of his recovery faded: Henry was dying. Helplessly, his grieving parents prayed continually as they watched their first child inching towards death. With all earthly hope gone, they spent most of one night in prayer, pleading with God for the life of their little one.

Changes came while they prayed. Henry began to

relax and soon he was sleeping contentedly. The fever had broken, and from that hour he began to recover.

Overwhelmed and exceedingly grateful to God for what he had done, the Whites decided to continue their work and travel for the cause of God. But what would they do with Henry? He was too frail for travel, so they decided not to take him with them.

Frances, daughter of Stockbridge Howland, offered to take care of Henry. That meant leaving the care of the baby in someone else's hands. They hesitated, yet, with a conviction of devotion to God and of a duty to his work, they finally accepted the suggestion.

The Howlands were by no means strangers to James and Ellen White. They were solid Christians and close friends. Their home was often referred to as 'Fort Howland' by early Adventists. Even so, leaving the baby, their only child, with someone else was almost too much for his mother.

A few months later, when the Whites were leaving, Henry was carried to the carriage to say goodbye. He was by then almost a year old and as Ellen White looked at him she saw sadness on his small face. As she bent down to kiss him, the thought that someone else would act a mother's part overwhelmed her. She burst into tears as the carriage drove away.

Although there were brief visits from his parents later, Henry stayed with the Howland family for the first five years of his life.

When he was six years old Henry was sick again and his parents rushed home to him. When he recovered, they decided to take him with them and that decision proved to be key for Henry's improved health. He became stronger and more vigorous from then on.

There were other times, however, when the Whites again left their children in the care of others, but their boys were never forgotten. Letters continually flowed between parents and children.

Here are parts of two letters Ellen White wrote to Henry. The first was addressed to all three boys, but one section of it was directed to Henry alone. He was working at the time in the Review and Herald building at Battle Creek, Michigan. The letter is dated 24 December 1857, which was when James and Ellen White were making a dangerous trip across the partly frozen Mississippi River in an open sleigh. They were on their way to Waukon, Iowa, and it was doubtful if they would reach their destination alive.

Here are Ellen White's thoughts towards Henry as she travelled. 'I hope, dear Henry, that you are a good boy, and are happy in doing right. Continue to strive to be faithful in all things. We received your letter, and were much pleased to hear from you. We think you have made improvements in setting type.'[1]

This was a mother thinking of her children and what they were doing while she was on an extremely risky journey in the middle of winter.

She closed the letter with words for all three of her boys. 'Trust in the Lord at all times. Listen to the voice of conscience. Love God and you will have his approving smile. What a thought, to have the Great God, the Maker of the heavens and the earth, to smile upon and love you. Dear children, seek for this, pray for it, live for it. Your affectionate Mother.'[2]

Another letter, dated 6 September 1859, two years later, was written directly to Henry. In part she wrote, 'We, your parents, pray much for you, that you may be a consistent, true Christian. We know that our Saviour is coming, and will take the good and holy, the honest and pure, to dwell with him forever in a holy heaven, where all is beauty, harmony, joy, and glory. I want you to remember that Jesus suffered, groaned, and died for you, that his blood might cleanse you from sin. But there is work for you to do. May the Lord clearly open to your young mind the plan of salvation, and lead you to give yourself unreservedly to Jesus as his.'[3]

In conclusion she added, 'Do right because you love to. Preserve these letters I write to you, and read them often, and if you should be left without a mother's care, they will be a help to you.' And once again she signed, 'Your affectionate Mother.'[4] She had no way of knowing then that in four short years it would be Henry who would die first.

The American Civil War raged in the south and east when Henry and James Edson were baptised together in the church at Battle Creek. It was in the winter following his fifteenth birthday that Henry was baptised.

But after that, something went terribly wrong. Satan had his hand on Henry and was pulling him in the wrong direction. The Whites lived in a house on Wood Street in Battle Creek and not far behind their home the state of Michigan built a racetrack. The excitement of horseracing and the thrill of the crowd appealed to Henry. Although there is no evidence that he ever attended a race, the influence was there just the same. It had a thrilling effect on his teenage mind.

That was also a time when young men were going to war. A draft-call from Abraham Lincoln was appealing for men who were just a little older than Henry. There was war talk in town, and a thrill of excitement and dread filled every home. Parades, bands, the sound of marching feet and cheering crowds pulled Henry in that direction.

Secretly, he and Edson left the house after supposedly going to bed each night to join the fun. Willie was too young for this and, although he knew what they were doing, he was silenced with threats from his older brothers not to tell. It was neighbours who told James and Ellen White what their boys were doing. Initially, they did not believe what they were told: their boys were not in town; they were home in bed. But the neighbours insisted they were right.

To prove them wrong, the Whites looked in on the boys one night after they had gone to bed. Two of them were gone, and a ground-floor window was open. Willie was the only one in the room: he was petrified with fear and would not tell where his brothers had gone.

The Whites sat down, looked at each other, and said, 'Where did we go wrong?'

They soon realised their mistake. They had left their boys on their own too much or in the care of other people, and they knew that it had to stop.

From then on, the Whites took their children with them when they travelled and never left them on their own again for long periods of time. The boys had duties such as providing music for meetings, ushering, or collecting offerings. Keeping them occupied ensured that they did not sit idly, but, unfortunately, the damage had already been done.

Insight into this situation can be found in a small book titled *An Appeal to the Youth,* which begins with a funeral address for Henry White, delivered by Uriah Smith. This is followed by a description of Henry's life and last sickness. The little volume ends with several pieces of Henry's favourite music and a few letters from Ellen White to her children.

Beginning on page 20 of that book, I will quote heavily from its pages.

'In the summer of 1863, [during the early part of the American Civil War] the parents made arrangements for a journey to New England . . . it was decided that they [Henry, Edson, and Willie] should accompany their parents.'[5]

Leaving Battle Creek on 19 August, the Whites made their first stop at Olcott, New York. 'In company with friends, the family enjoyed a boat ride on Lake Ontario. Henry [who had a tenor voice] and his brothers sang "The Evergreen Shore" and several other pieces.'[6] Both boys were quite musical. Needless to say, they had a great time together.

The main reason for that trip east was for James White to negotiate for a series of charts on Bible prophecies and the Ten Commandments. From Olcott the family travelled to New York and then to Boston where work on the charts took place.

While in Boston, friends of the family took the

boys on tours of the city. They visited several well-known places of interest such as the Bunker Hill Monument, Prospect Hill, the State House and other sites. The boys were having fun.

'From Boston the family went to Topsham, Maine. Here, at his old home, Henry was affectionately and joyfully welcomed by those who had formerly cared for him.'[7] And to the delight of Henry and Edson, a melodeon, a small reed organ, was bought for them to enjoy.

At that point James and Ellen White left their children in the care of the Howland family as they departed for meetings in New Hampshire, Vermont and New York State. The boys went to the depot to see them off, 'and, before the family parted, Henry, Edson and Willie, by request, sang "The Evergreen Shore", much to the gratification of the crowd waiting for another train. The whistle was heard, the "goodbye" and "farewell" were said, and away sped the train, bearing the parents on their mission of love, and leaving the children again without their watch-care.'[8]

That was something they had said they would not do, but they did.

While in Brookfield, New York, James White had a dream that things were going wrong in Topsham with the boys. Mail from Maine reported that things were fine and that nothing was wrong, but that did not satisfy the Whites. Concern took over and, as soon as their business ended, they were on a train speeding towards Topsham.

'The day before they reached Topsham, Henry

came in from his work in the afternoon, and threw himself upon the sofa, and said that he never felt such a gloom resting upon his mind before in all his life. He said that it was not anything he had done which caused such feelings, but that it seemed to him that something dreadful was about to happen.'[9]

The following day the Whites arrived and all three boys were there to meet them. 'When the cars stopped, Henry bounded through the crowd with more than usual activity, and embraced his mother most affectionately, while in her heart she thanked God for such a son.'[10]

When they arrived back at the Howlands' home, Henry wanted to play and sing one of his favourite pieces for them, 'Home Again'.[11]

'In four days from this time, which was December 1st, he was taken sick. . . . He failed rapidly.'[12]

Uriah Smith in the *Review and Herald* magazine for 15 December 1863 stated that Henry's sickness was lung fever. Today Henry's sickness might have been diagnosed as pneumonia.

Henry was taken from his room on the second floor and carried to one of the lower front rooms. It was the same room where 'sixteen years before, when but an infant, he was apparently brought to the point of death.'[13]

On the following day, 2 December, his mother told him that persons violently attacked as he had been were frequently deprived of their reason, and if he had anything to say, he had better improve the present opportunity. He said that he felt unprepared to die, and requested his parents pray for him. After they prayed for him, he called his brothers to him. He embraced them, and told them he had not always treated them as a brother should have done, and wept as he asked their forgiveness.[14]

Tears flowed freely as they hugged one another.

In the evening he requested that all the family should have a praying session in his room.[15] He feared that because of his past God would not look on him with favour. He was assured that Christ came to save those like him and was encouraged to rely on him. To this Henry said, 'Oh Lord, forgive my sins, and accept me as Thine.' He then repeated these words several times, 'Here, Lord, I give myself away, 'Tis all that I can do.'[16]

Henry's concern was that he had not cultivated a better Christian character and had been a poor example to others. He wanted to get well to show gratitude to his parents and be a true Christian. He also wanted to be a blessing to his young friends and other teens. He dictated a message for them, saying that 'The death-bed is a poor place to prepare for an inheritance in the second life. Spend the best years of your days in serving the Lord.'[17] And especially to his young friends in Battle Creek he added, 'Don't take my life for an example! Give up the world and be Christians.'[18]

A sense of relief and comfort followed his confessions; he felt a closeness to the Lord and was assured of forgiveness for sins. He openly praised the Lord for his goodness.

On 3 December blood was discharged from his mouth and nose. He had no desire to live and asked his mother to promise him that if he died he might be taken to Battle Creek, 'and laid by the side of my little brother, John Herbert, that we may come up together in the morning of the resurrection.'[19]

He also told his mother that he often felt she was too hard on him. 'But,' he said, 'Mother, you have not been any too strict. I now realise that I was in danger, and am glad you said as much as you did. I wish I had heeded your advice more faithfully.'[20]

From then on he grew weaker and could speak only in whispers.

James began to fall apart. On 5 December he found a place by himself and poured out his heart to God for his son. He returned to Henry and assured him that God would do all things well, and Henry responded, 'Yes, he will.'[21]

He told his father that if he died he would escape being drafted into the Civil War. That, and going through the seven last plagues, had weighed heavily on his mind.

His father was with him for most of 7 December and Henry didn't want him to leave. Then, as Henry's mind began to wander, his father held him in his arms while he prayed and tried to soothe and comfort him. Henry's mind revived, but he would not let his father go for a minute. There was great affection as James continued to hold his son tightly.

That incident reveals a side of James White that was seldom witnessed. He is usually thought of as a man possessing a stern, strict, unemotional and serious nature. But here we find him tenderly holding his son in his arms and shedding tears of deep sorrow. This shows great compassion and is indicative of a warm, loving, caring nature. Here, then, was a person determined, at all costs, to do God's will and, at the same time, able to love people with a tenderness and an anxiety that a true Christian should possess.

A short time before his death on 8 December, Henry said to his mother, 'Mother, I shall meet you in heaven in the morning of the resurrection, for I know you will be there.'[22]

His last words were, 'Heaven is sweet.'[23]

Ellen White had now lost two of her four sons, her first born and her youngest.

References

[1] *An Appeal to the Youth*, page 41, published by the Steam Press of the Seventh-day Adventist Publishing Association, Battle Creek, Michigan, 1864.
[2] *Ibid*.
[3] *Ibid*, page 46.
[4] *Ibid*, page 47.
[5] *Ibid*, pages 20-21.
[6] *Ibid*, page 21.
[7] *Ibid*, page 22.
[8] *Ibid*, pages 22-23.
[9] *Ibid*, page 23.
[10] *Ibid*, pages 23-24.
[11-14] *Ibid*, page 24.
[15-16] *Ibid*, page 25.
[17-18] *Ibid*, page 28.
[19-20] *Ibid*, page 26.
[21] *Ibid*, page 27.
[22-23] *Ibid*, page 31.

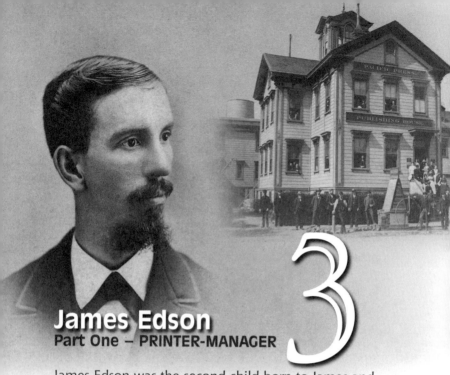

James Edson
Part One – PRINTER-MANAGER

James Edson was the second child born to James and Ellen White. He entered the world in July 1849 at Rocky Hill, Connecticut, and he, like his brother Henry, became talented in music.

As an adult Edson was five feet nine inches tall and had big ears which made his eyes look smaller than they really were. He also had a long nose. On top of that, he wore gold-rimmed glasses, but most people didn't notice, because they seemed to suit his face. He looked good anyway.

In 1852 the Whites were living in Rochester, New York. James Edson was three years old, and in a letter written to the Howland family on 16 April, Ellen White describes her family's living conditions.

'We have rented an old house,' she wrote, 'for one hundred and seventy-five dollars a year. We have the [printing] press in the house. Were it not for this, we should have to pay fifty dollars a year for office room.'[1]

Mrs White went on to describe their furniture: two old bedsteads which cost twenty-five cents; six old chairs that didn't match and four more chairs without seats bought for one dollar and sixty-two cents respectively.

Food was a real problem; as they didn't have much money, turnips became their potatoes. Their kitchen table was a wooden board laid across two empty flour barrels.

Cholera struck the city, and Ellen wrote that, 'all night long the carriages bearing the dead were heard rumbling through the streets.'[2] Children were very susceptible to disease in the 1800s and three-year-old Edson came down with the cholera. 'I took him in my arms,' wrote his mother, 'and in the name of Jesus rebuked the disease. He felt relief at once.'[3]

Others were praying for him, and while they were doing so Edson 'looked up in astonishment, and said in his tiny voice, "They need not pray any more, for the Lord has healed me."'[4] But as he recovered, he would not eat and this became a problem, not only for the health of the child but for the Whites as well. Two months of travel and appointments faced them and they didn't know what to do.

Again she wrote, 'We hardly dared to leave the child [with someone else] in so critical a state, but decided to go unless there was a change for the worse.'[5] They planned to leave in two days.

They prayed, saying that if Edson would eat, it would be a sign they were to leave. Nothing happened the first day but, after their prayer on the second day, Edson was hungry.

'We began our journey,' wrote Ellen White, 'that afternoon. About four o'clock I took my sick child upon a pillow, and we rode twenty miles. He seemed very nervous that night. He could not sleep, and I held him in my arms nearly the whole night.'[6]

A decision had to be made the following morning as to whether they should go on or turn back. The people with whom they were staying warned them that, if they travelled on, Edson would die.

They decided to go anyway, believing the sickness to be Satan's attempt to stop their work for the Lord. 'I said to my husband,' stated Ellen White, 'If we go back, I shall expect the child to die. He can but die if we go forward. Let us proceed on our journey, trusting in the Lord.'[7]

They travelled in a covered carriage with their favourite horse Charlie and expected to cover a hundred miles in two days. As they went on, Ellen White commented, 'I was much exhausted, and feared I should fall asleep and let the child fall from my arms; so I laid him upon my lap, and tied him to my waist, and we both slept that day over much of the distance.'[8]

Edson made a complete recovery.

There are snippets of the Whites' early home life with their boys to be found mostly in letters. But in a copy of the *Review and Herald* magazine for 13 February 1936, Willie wrote about his early home life, which, of course, would include references to Edson. Describing a community well, he said, 'I well remember clearly its wooden curb and windlass and its oaken bucket, and how good the water tasted to thirsty boys.'[9] (A windlass is a device for raising or hauling objects, usually by a crank, lever, or motor. In this case it was a hand crank.)

The daily routine went something like this: 'At six o'clock all were up. Often mother had been writing for two or three hours, and the cook had been busy in the kitchen since five o'clock. By six-thirty breakfast was ready.'[10] Conversation at the table sometimes involved what Ellen White had written that morning, what work James was doing at the Review and Herald office or other church interests.

Willie continued. 'At seven o'clock all assembled in the parlour for morning worship. Father would read, . . . with comments, and then lead in the morning song. . . . The hymn most frequently used was:

> *Lord, in the morning Thou shalt hear*
> *My voice ascending high;*
> *To Thee will I direct my prayer,*
> *To Thee lift up mine eye.*

'Then Father prayed. He did not just offer a prayer; he prayed with earnestness and with solemn reverence . . . To us children, who grew up in the atmosphere of reverence and prayer, this was the common routine.'[11]

When James White was away, his wife took over, and if both were away, the person in charge of the house conducted the service. 'The worship hour was as regularly observed as the hours for breakfast and dinner.'[12]

Four boys in the White House

Following this activity, James left for work. 'After father left the house, mother enjoyed spending half an hour in her flower garden, . . . her children were encouraged to work with her.'[13] After the gardening, she would spend several hours writing again.

'Her afternoons were usually occupied with . . . sewing, mending, knitting, darning, and working in her flower garden.'[14] In addition, there were trips to town and visits to the sick.

Between seven and eight in the evening, 'the whole family would assemble for worship, . . . Father, if present, read a chapter from the Bible and prayed, thanking God for the blessings of the day, and committing the family to God's care for the night.'[15]

Ellen White's diary entry of Sabbath 19 March 1859 reads, 'Tarried at home in the afternoon. Read to my children.'[16] That didn't happen only on Sabbath. Both parents read to their children frequently and James saw that a large supply of books was on hand at all times.

In a letter Willie wrote to Hannah Jones on 9 December 1934, he mentioned that much of his school years were interrupted with travel and by his father's illness. He also stated that when he was about six years old, one teacher, Adelia Patten, came to the house to teach the Whites' boys. This included Henry and Edson.

In another letter to F. F. Byington, dated 4 February 1935, Willie said that when he was in Battle Creek he attended public school No. 3 for a while. Henry and Edson were both taught by Will Byington, principal and teacher for the higher grades, in classroom number 4; Willie went to room number 2.

When he was 15 Edson worked for the Review and Herald and it was there he mastered the printer's trade. In a letter written to Grace Amadon, dated 19 April 1935, Willie wrote about work at the Review. He referred to 'when Edson mailed.' (This mailing could mean Edson wrapped packages for mailing.) 'I was employed to sit on a table cross-legged like a tailor and gather up the pages and even and stack them ready for wrapping. When I was 13 and Edson 18, . . . Edson set the type and did the press work on the old Washington hand press and I was roller boy.' Being a roller involved rolling ink across the type, making it ready for the press to receive and print one sheet of paper at a time.

Willie added an amusing insight. 'As molasses and glue,' he said, 'were chief ingredients in the manufacture of the rollers, the younger boys around the office [the Press] formed the habit of chewing the roller material because of its sweetness!'[17]

All three of Ellen and James White's boys worked in the printing trade.

On 28 July 1870, aged 21, Edson married Emma MacDearmon and soon afterwards the newlyweds headed west.

Edson had been asked to take charge of the newly formed Pacific SDA Publishing Association in Oakland, California. This establishment is still in operation today, presently located in Nampa, Idaho, and known as the Pacific Press Publishing Association.

Edson held the top position as plant business manager for three years but that was a rough time for him and Emma. Money was scarce and, to make ends meet, he worked a couple of days a week setting music for firms in San Francisco, earning between five and eight dollars a day this way. He also hoped Emma would be able to find work at a place called Tay's store. After telling Willie about that, and to avoid questions from his brother, he added in a letter dated 4 January 1875, 'I only work a day or two per week at it, as I will not neglect the work at the office.'[18]

In another letter to his brother dated 5 July 1874, Edson wrote, 'Oakland is a fine place. Very aristocratic. Property is very high here. My place, as near town as it is there, would bring $5,000. Would rent for $35 to $40 per month . . . I tell you, it costs to turn around here.'[19]

In the 16 September 1875 issue of the *Review and Herald* magazine we are given an insight into what was happening at the newly established Pacific Press.

'For some time our rented rooms,' wrote Edson, 'on the corner of Twelfth and Broadway were much too small for the carrying on of the work of the *Signs of the Times* [for which the business was founded], with any degree of comfort. Hence we have for several weeks been regarding with no small degree of interest the progress of the carpenters who were erecting the new office [building] on Castro Street between Eleventh and Twelfth.'[20]

Edson (known to many as J. E.) was overseeing the construction of a new building to house the publishing work, namely, the printing of the *Signs of the Times*, and it was no easy task. There was a shortage of money, and many Adventists in California grew sceptical of the project.

But, being young and enthusiastic, Edson had high hopes for the success of the business. He continued: 'By an effort on the part of carpenters, plasterers, and painters, two commodious rooms were completed before the rest of the building, and pronounced ready for occupancy.'[21] Edson must have been pushing some of the workmen to work harder and faster. 'Friday, August 27, which day was devoted to moving material and getting ready for the work of the coming week.'[22]

Edson asked that the new building be dedicated before any work should begin. He harked back to its shaky beginning by saying, 'It was started in a very humble manner in two small rented rooms on the second floor. Now, we were to commence work in perhaps the finest office building upon the Pacific Coast.'[23]

Picture the scene. '. . . last Sunday morning as we were about to commence work, all hands, including carpenters, painters and printers, assembled in the type-room while Brother Charles Jones read the second chapter of Titus and offered a prayer for the blessing of God upon the work carried on, and upon the hands engaged in the work.'[24]

Thus began the official work of Pacific Press.

Soon after that, the Whites made a trip to California. Edson was overjoyed and wanted to show them everything about the new plant. In a letter he said, 'I took them from room to room and explained the arrangement and working of every department.'[25]

As they entered the editorial room, they found it empty and this is what happened. 'Mother turned to me and said, "I was shown your work in putting this office in order, and was shown an angel of God going by your side into every room you entered, and with every task you undertook."'[26] Edson was stunned.

But trouble was about to raise its ugly head.

Skilled workmen were scarce on the West Coast. Edson called for help from Battle Creek, but it was like shouting in the dark. Few, if any, answered his call and he was forced to employ non-Adventists. The pay was low; he could not possibly compete with the higher wages paid by similar businesses across the bay in San Francisco. Also, the quality of work from those he hired was poor.

For a first-hand report of those early days and what Edson had to deal with, we turn to one of his letters.

'The editing,' he wrote concerning the *Signs of the Times*, 'was placed upon me, a youngster of 23 or 24 years. We had one typewriter. I was in full charge. The correspondence, the looking after finances, the mailing lists, and whatever business came with the work. The folding of the papers [mainly the *Signs of the Times*], the addressing the wrappers and mailing the papers, fell upon my wife and myself. For this we jointly received $12.00 a week, in perhaps the most expensive of cities in all the U.S. We lived in one room adjoining the type room.'[27]

Not long after that, a building was constructed, and a large press arrived from his father, who was in the east, but no one knew how to work the machine.

'I clamped my teeth and went over to San Francisco,' he wrote, 'And after several refusals found a fine printer with a Hoe Cylinder who would allow me to bring the forms of the *Signs* to his office, feed the press myself, and pay him full price for the presswork. I paid the express charges for shipping type forms to and from San Francisco, and my own extra expenses. On the other hand, I collected only the price we had been paying for having the presswork done in Oakland.'[28]

He went on to say that that process had to stop. Pacific Press owned a great new stream press in Oakland with no one to run it. It lay scattered in several pieces, so Edson decided to cross the bay to search the city of San Francisco for someone who knew how to run it.

He located two men who promised to do the work, but they never came.

Edson continued: '. . . I sought the Lord for wisdom, and then ordered steam up in the engine room and went to work. We had a man as engineer who was handy, and we went at it. There were several glaring mistakes in adjusting the press. It took us a full day before all parts did their duty, and at the right time.

'We inked up and put in the rollers, and I climbed up to the feed board and it took two or three hours to get acquainted with the anatomy of that great nickel-plated monster. The floor was then strewn with sheets of paper spoiled, and then I began really to feed. We had no further difficulty with it, and never did we have to go outside for our pressman.'[29]

Edson and Emma returned to Battle Creek, Michigan, in the autumn of 1880. Once there, he busied himself in the newly developing Sabbath School work and while attending a series on Sabbath School development, he was elected vice-president. He continued in that position for six years, serving occasionally on the executive and publishing committees. He was also chairman of the lesson committee and was prominent in launching the church publication, *Sabbath School Worker.* In 1886 he helped to publish the church's second Sabbath School songbook titled *Joyful Greetings for the Sabbath School.*

In the 1880s and 90s Edson created his own publishing company with agents selling books on etiquette, cooking and business forms.

The General Conference of 1886 turned to Edson, F. E. Belden, and Edwin Barnes for the production and development of a church hymnbook. It was titled *Hymns and Tunes.* Edson's company, the J. E. White Publishing Company, set the type for the music and words.

It was about that time, the late 1880s and early 1890s, that Edson extended his business to Chicago.

Little could he have realised it, but Edson would soon come face to face with a dramatic situation which was to change his life forever.

References

[1] Ellen G. White, *Life Sketches*, page 142, (Pacific Press Publishing Association).

[2] *Ibid*, page 143.

[3-6] *Ibid*, page 144.

[7-8] *Ibid*, page 145.

[9-15] *Review and Herald* magazine, 13 February 1936. (Review and Herald Publishing Association).

[16] *Review and Herald* magazine, 27 February 1936. (Review and Herald Publishing Association).

[17] *Spirit of Prophecy Emphasis Week for Seventh-day Adventist Schools*, 1972-3, (Ellen G. White Estate), pages 27-28.

[18] Letter dated Oakland, California, 4 January 1875 from James Edson White to his brother, Willie. Original letter in the Ellen G. White Estate in Washington, D.C. (C. H. Jones file).

[19] Letter dated Oakland, California, 5 July 1874 from James Edson White to his brother Willie. Original in the E. G. White Estate (C. H. Jones file).

[20-24] *Review and Herald* magazine, 16 September 1875, (Review and Herald Publishing), page 88.

[25-29] Letter to A. G. Daniells from James Edson White, Battle Creek, Michigan, 9 March 1920. Original in the E. G. White Estate, Washington D.C.

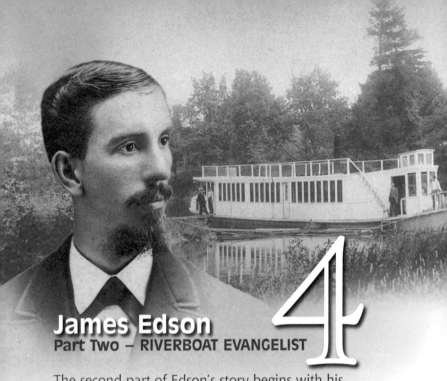

James Edson
Part Two – RIVERBOAT EVANGELIST

The second part of Edson's story begins with his mother. Ellen White gave a speech about the Seventh-day Adventist Church and the African Americans in the southern United States. In it she stated that the Church was not doing much for them in the way of education, pointing out that they needed to learn to read and write. Also, no one was telling them the Gospel of Jesus Christ and she stressed that something should be done about it. Her speech was published under the title of *Our Duty to the Coloured People.*

Ellen White's appeal was presented on 21 March 1891.[1] The American Civil War had been over for thirty years, yet nothing was being done to help these people. What she said and wrote had fallen on deaf ears.

Most of those African Americans had been former

slaves. There were thousands of them, their vast numbers adding up to a nation within a nation.

Edson was interested, but he was unaware of what his mother had said, and no one could tell him. Then, by chance, he found a copy of his mother's printed message lying among papers scattered on the floor of an empty office room at the Review and Herald building in Battle Creek.

After reading it, he asked his wife, Emma, 'Why don't we do something?' Then, 'Why don't *I* do something?'[2]

Forty-four-year-old Edson determined to go to those people with the Gospel. He would search for them, tell them the story of Jesus and also teach them how to read and write. Emma agreed.

In a letter to his mother in 1894, Edson wrote about Emma's attitude towards the project: 'The thing which does me as much good as anything else is the cheerful, hopeful, helpful spirit Emma manifests. She is ready to do anything that is best and duty. She will go south with me in the spring and take hold with me in teaching and assisting the coloured people.'[3]

He was warned that many white people in the southern states would try to stop his work, especially those living along the Mississippi and Yazoo Rivers. They advised that he would not only be unwelcome but he would also be unable to find a place to live.

Edson had a ready answer for that: he would build a boat. Not only would it provide him and Emma with a place to live but it would also be powerful enough to sail up and down the great rivers. Besides that, it would be a schoolhouse and a church.

Friends rallied to help him build. To raise funds, he went into financial partnership with W. O. Palmer. The initial cost was $3,700.[3] By 1896 Edson had managed to buy out Palmer's share, making him sole owner of the vessel.[4]

There was feverish activity with construction and a great amount of work, almost too much. But little by little the boat began to take shape, and when it was finally completed he named it the *Morning Star.* A company in Chicago even donated an organ for church meetings.

The vessel was twelve feet wide and seventy-two feet long, with a small house sitting on top of it. A boiler room supplied steam for a large paddlewheel that pushed the boat along and there were five other rooms, even space for an office and a printing press. The deck was large enough to accommodate two hundred people. Below deck was an ice chest that held a ton of ice. Solid Michigan oak, two-and-a-half inches thick, was used for building, and over a ton of bolts and spikes were needed to hold everything together.

The boat was constructed on dry land in the middle of the state of Michigan, a long way from the Mississippi River, but this was no problem for Edson. He knew of a small river that ran close by called the Kalamazoo which emptied into Lake Michigan. The *Morning Star* would have no trouble sailing those waters.

Edson made arrangements for a tugboat to meet them when they reached Lake Michigan. The tug was named the *Bon Ami* and was strong enough to pull everything across the lake by a 200-foot cable.

However, there was trouble right from the start. When the tug began its work, a howling storm struck which almost swamped it and threatened to sink the *Morning Star.*

Lake Michigan is like an inland ocean – big, deep and cold – and so vast that no one standing on the shoreline can see the other side. It can become wildly dangerous and there are hundreds of ships resting on its bed.

But Edson was determined that no storm or lake was going to stop him. Furniture was lashed down with ropes to save it from washing overboard. Giant waves pounded them; water poured over the decks and raced through doors into rooms; time after time the *Morning Star* was tossed high into the air and then plunged downward. Emma, aboard the *Bon Ami,* covered her head and prayed. All the men on the *Morning Star* were seasick. But the cable held.

God was with Edson's boat that day: his protecting hand was over them all the time as finally they sailed into the port of Chicago. It took a few days for the crew to recover and for things to dry out and then it was off to the great Mississippi River.

They travelled by the Illinois and Michigan Canal to LaSalle. From there they sailed down the Illinois River to the Mississippi, arriving at Vicksburg on 10 January 1895.[5]

By that time the boat had picked up six new crewmembers, but she was too small and there was no room for them.

That, again, was no problem for Edson; he and Palmer simply traded tools for a sunken, flat-bottomed barge, ninety feet wide and forty-two feet long. They had it re-floated, built a small house on top and towed it behind the *Star* and named it *Dawn.*

Everything was ready when the small fleet of two boats reached the Mississippi. All aboard the *Star* and *Dawn* knew that God had been with them every wet mile of the way and that he would never leave them.

In those days the Mississippi River was a giant water highway, equivalent to motorways today. It flows from Canada down to the south of the United States, emptying into the Gulf of Mexico. Besides great numbers of large and small riverboats parting the water, there were flat-bottomed barges and giant paddle-wheeled passenger ships with several decks. Even rafts rode the river currents.

Everything went by water. Riverboats transported such things as fire engines, ploughs, oxen, bricks, wood, cows, farm tools, and even entire sawmills. You name it – the boats had it. Some passenger boats even hauled cattle, horses, chickens, ducks, turkeys and sheep. The smell and noise passengers would have been forced to endure must have been extremely unpleasant.

The *Morning Star* travelled between ten and twelve miles an hour, covering about a hundred to a hundred and twenty-five miles a day.

Once they reached the Mississippi, Edson and the *Morning Star* crew faced many problems. One was dealing with government officials. There was a law which demanded that all boats on the river must have a licensed pilot on board. (A pilot would know the river well and his licence gave him the right to guide boats safely on the water.) When the *Morning Star* reached the city of Cairo, Illinois, no pilot was to be found, so they could go no farther.

As a frantic search was made to find a pilot, a black teenager appeared, looking for work. His name was Finis Parker and he offered to help locate a pilot for them. But, even with his help, no pilot was found.

Their disappointment turned to surprise when all aboard the *Star* heard Finis claim to know every inch of the river, and could pilot them himself. Despite the fact that he was black, underage and had no licence, Edson hired him.

Finis, true to his word, climbed into the pilothouse and guided the boat past dangerous places such as sandbars and shallow water, always keeping the *Star* in deep water. He knew what he was doing. Whenever another boat appeared, Finis would duck out of sight and someone else would take over the wheel until it passed.

A year later, Finis was old enough for a licence, and Edson tried to persuade government authorities in Saint Louis to issue Finis with one but they refused because he was black.

That kind of attitude was one reason why Edson had taken on the project; he wanted to change things. Contrary to popular opinion, he believed that black and white people were all God's children; Jesus died for each and every one of them.

Four boys in the White House

In 1894, when the *Morning Star* anchored near Vicksburg, Mississippi, the area around the city still had evidence of the fierce fighting that had gone on during the war. Miles of trenches could be seen where soldiers had tried to hide; cannonballs, bullets and fragments of bullets were everywhere.

Thousands of people, both black and white, lived in the area and it was there that Edson and the *Morning Star* found their first students. Not all of them were children; middle-aged and older people came. There were so many wanting to learn that night-school classes were started.

More seats were needed, so, instead of individual chairs, Edson made benches which would accommodate four or more people. Still that wasn't enough and many sat on the floor and used seats for desks, while others just stretched out on the deck.

The first and most important thing those people wanted to learn was how to write. So, along with reading came spelling, arithmetic, handwriting and grammar classes. Edson and Emma taught boys, girls, grandmothers and grandfathers. Bible studies were added for extra work after school. Years later, some of those very students became Seventh-day Adventist preachers and teachers.

When public Bible meetings were started, black boys and girls distributed handbills which had been printed on the small printing press aboard the boat. Many who came to the meetings stated the thing they enjoyed most was the singing.

'Antie' Miller, a very old ex-slave, had this to say: 'I learned to read at White's school. I was 'bout fifty years old. Never had a chance to read nor nothing. But I started, an' in a month I could read, but I couldn't understand. I used to cry over it, but then Sister White [Emma], she's a blessed woman, she'd encourage me. Come sit down beside me, she would an' help me. An' in two months I could read an' I could understand. Sister White sure was a good woman. An' she could sing. Brother White an' she certainly could sing. They sang good together. I reckon she was the best singer that ever went out.'[6]

But there were times when trouble arose. Edson was threatened by a mob of white people who said they would hang him if he continued his work. White people teaching blacks made them angry. Many wanted ex-slaves to remain ignorant as this would ensure cheap labour. They reasoned that if those people were educated, they would claim higher wages. They certainly didn't want that to happen.

When such threats occurred, Edson would pull up anchor and sail the *Morning Star* to the next landing. Then, when the trouble died down in the place he had left, he would pull up anchor again and sail back. Never once did he stop preaching and teaching.

It was certainly not all peace and quiet. One of the *Morning Star* helpers, a man named Rogers, was shot at while on his way home one evening. The bullets missed him, but two went through his hat. The next day he discovered that a number of black men had lain hidden around his home all night to protect him.

At another time, an angry mob tried to burn down

a small church the *Morning Star* people had built at Yazoo City. Rushing to the building, they set it on fire, then yelling and hollering they ran away. But for some unknown reason, as the mob ran off, the flames in the church suddenly went out. The building survived, and the worshippers gave credit for it to the Lord.

One day, to the surprise of everyone working on the boat, they saw, walking towards them out of a cypress swamp, a husband and wife. Edson welcomed them warmly and invited them aboard. Then, to the shock of all, that couple told everyone they were keeping the Sabbath.

'How did this happen?' Emma asked.

They explained that they had read about the true Sabbath from a small printed paper. That pamphlet had been printed aboard the *Morning Star* and one of the ship's workers had handed it to them.

Next, there was more surprise for everyone, as the couple handed Edson twenty dollars in nickels and dimes. It was their tithe money.[7]

Ellen White paid a visit to Edson and Emma on the *Morning Star.* She wanted to know first-hand what her son and daughter-in-law were doing. She stayed a week, during which time she observed them closely. She saw them give food and clothing to those who had none; she listened while they spoke comforting words to the sad. She also took note of students, many of whom had walked miles to attend, coming to the boat after putting in a hard day's work. They needed encouragement and sympathy. Emma and Edson gave help to all who came.

It was that visit to the southern states that made Ellen White aware of the desperate need to enlarge a small school, Oakwood Manual Training School in Alabama, and, because of her urging, that was done. Later, as the school began to grow, it was renamed Oakwood College. It had been created for the education of African Americans and still functions today.

Ellen White made a statement confirming that it makes no difference to God whether people are black, white, brown, yellow or red: they are all his children.

Before leaving the *Morning Star,* she encouraged her son with the words, 'Angels of God look on with approval.'[8]

Emma and Edson fought sickness most of the time they worked in the south, the damp climate never agreeing with either of them. The bouts of malaria were especially bad, leaving them both weak, although Emma suffered more acutely. Edson also had a terrible accident that left him with intense headaches for the rest of his life. One night he was caught in a severe storm and the resultant poor visibility caused him to stumble and trip. He fell, hitting his head on a pile of lumber. The accident left him dazed for weeks.

He said, 'I thought every muscle was torn loose, and my neck broken.'[9] He suffered a considerable loss of blood.

While those things drained the couple's strength, they never gave up on their work with those they had come to help, the impoverished and illiterate, many of whom were so poor they earned less than fifty cents a week. The Whites also had to contend with those who wanted the African Americans to remain poor and uneducated. Despite the constant pressures, Edson and Emma kept on working.

Did all their time, money spent, and effort pay off? Was it worth it? If reckoned in pecuniary terms, the answer is 'No.' But if it is counted in the number of lives touched by the love of God; if it is in teaching people the basic essentials of learning to enable them to live a better life, the answer is 'Yes.'

Eventually, however, ill health forced Edson and Emma to stop their work on the river. They had done their very best. As the years rolled by, others with boats like theirs took their place. More than fifty mission boats took up where the *Morning Star* left off. Some, but not all, were run by Seventh-day Adventists, but that was not important. The job Edson began was done: the *Morning Star* had sailed into its last port, making way for others and the rise of a glorious new dawn.

What did some of those African Americans think of Edson White?

Here's the opinion of Joe Miller, an elderly man. (He was discussing Edson White with Arthur Spalding, a leading minister of the Seventh-day Adventist Church.) Miller and his wife, 'Antie', had a picture of the Whites on a wall in their home. Joe heard that Edson had stopped briefly in their town on business and that he would be leaving on the train that same night.

Joe, anxious to see his old friend, said, 'I can't see

him then, 'less maybe if I'll stay at the station this evening.'[10]

And that is just what he did.

'By and by he came in with another white gentleman. He walked right past me.'[11] 'I touched him on the arm,' he said. 'He dropped his grip [on his suitcase] and grabbed me. Like to knock me down. We sat down and talked till he plumb had to get up on the train.'[12]

Evidently there had been people at the station watching Joe and Edson. Joe continued with his story. 'After he was gone,' he said, 'some white people came by and said, "Miller, who was that old man? Look like he love you so."

'I said, "Well, I do love him."

"Well, who was it?"

"Oh, that's Brother White."

"What? That old Adventist preacher [who] used to be here?"

"Sure, that's the one, I said. But I don't reckon I'll never see him no more."'[13]

There are those who believe that Edson founded Oakwood College in Alabama but that was not the case. He did, however, found the Southern Missionary Society to teach literacy and the Gospel story to ex-slaves and other African Americans in the southern states.

Yet there is one connection between Oakwood College and the *Morning Star.* The *Star* burned out in 1906. There was a metal star attached to it somewhere as a symbol of its name. That survived the fire and was rescued along with the ship's bell and taken to Oakwood College. On arrival, the star was placed on one of the school buildings, serving as a reminder to students of the *Morning Star* and of a man who followed a dream that involved a once enslaved race of people whom he deeply loved. That love never diminished and the people knew it.

That star is gone today, yet the memory of it shines as brightly as ever. Some people may forget about that star and the man it stood for, but God never will. Its glow will continue to shine brighter and brighter as long as time shall last.

Edson published a small monthly paper aboard the *Morning Star*. The first edition, issued in Yazoo City, Mississippi, and dated May 1898, carried the title, *The Gospel Herald*, and a banner ran through the heading with the words, 'Peace on Earth, Good Will Toward Men.'[14]

The main article on the front page gave a history of the *Morning Star*, its *raison d'être* and its work. There was also a detailed description of the boat, including its initial cost, the workers involved, the size and function of each room, its owner and his purpose and aim in building it. There were also three woodcuts of the boat and the barge called *Dawn*.

The last paragraph of the article is found on page two and reads as follows:

'The *Morning Star* is officered by God-fearing men. Her owner carries papers from the government as master and pilot and also an engineer. As he is not allowed to perform the duties of more than one office at a time, a pilot has been secured, who, from a wicked river man has, since coming upon it, been thoroughly converted to God through the influence of the boat. Her crew, except on some special occasions, is made up of missionary workers, and all upon the boat have but one aim and desire, to see sinners turn to God and be fully saved in his Kingdom.'[15]

In order to procure sufficient funds to continue his missionary work, Edson began writing books – twelve in all. Among them were *Best Stories From the Best Book* (still in print in 1965); *Past, Present, and Future;* and *The Coming King.* His books were sold in the hundreds of thousands, many being translated into other languages.

Edson was also instrumental in creating a publishing company in Nashville, Tennessee. It almost went bankrupt, yet survived and later became the start of the Southern Publishing Association, owned and operated by the Seventh-day Adventist denomination.

In 1912, because of Emma's poor health, the couple moved to Marshall, Michigan, where she died on 29 July 1917. Following that, Edson resettled in Battle Creek and started a business making stereopticon slides, mainly for missionaries and their work.

On 13 August 1922 he married Rebecca Burrill. The couple moved to Otsego, Michigan, where, on 30 May 1928, Edson died.

No one has the complete story of what happened during those early days, as Edson's letters, of which parts have been quoted, are, of course, partial and reveal only *his* view of events. One thing is certain, however. James Edson White was a good man, a true, honest pioneer in the cause he loved so dearly, the work of spreading the Three Angels' Messages and the Seventh-day Adventist Church.

In retirement, Edson had time to reflect on his past. He never met a girl named Anna Knight, but he knew there had to be others like her out there somewhere, and he had been determined to find them. He often recalled the days when black boys and girls, grandmothers and grandfathers sprawled out on the deck of the *Morning Star,* learning the hard lessons of reading and writing. It was there he found his Anna Knights. Some were boys, too, who would rise to leadership in the cause of their Lord and Master, Jesus Christ.

Who was Anna Knight? She was a brilliant black girl who became a source of pride to her race.

Anna was born in Mississippi in 1874, when education for black children was non-existent. When Sundays came around, she often played with white children in the neighbourhood, and as she did so she listened to them read and spell. She learned both subjects quickly, but had no materials with which to write, so she made the best of the resources she had. She practised writing by clearing a patch of ground and then scratching words on it with a stick. By the time she reached her teens, she had mastered the skills of learning taught in schools around her, although she had never once stepped inside a school building.

Shortly after that, Anna wrote to a New England newspaper asking for something to read and her request was published. A reader promptly sent Anna the *Signs of the Times* and it was largely due to this magazine that she was converted to the Seventh-day Adventist Church.

In 1884, a church conference worker in Tennessee helped her to enrol in Mount Vernon Academy and in 1898 she graduated from Battle Creek College as a nurse. Returning to Mississippi, she operated a self-supporting school for black children in Jasper County.

Anna's story does not end there. In 1901 she went to India for six years as a missionary. In 1909 she was called to the South-eastern Union in Atlanta, Georgia, where her duties were nursing, teaching, and Bible work. She later served in the Educational Department.

Anna wrote her life story in the book *The Mississippi Girl.* At the age of 98 she became president of the National Coloured Teachers' Association. Anna was also awarded the Medallion Merit Award for extraordinary meritorious service to Seventh-day Adventist education.[16]

We return to the subject of Oakwood College and its early days. In 1895, upon Ellen White's urging, a committee of three men found themselves walking through 360 acres of weeds on the grounds of a run-down southern plantation near Huntsville, Alabama. Their remit was to spend no more than $8,000 on land to start a school for black young people. This was to become Oakwood College and the three gentlemen were O. A. Olsen, president of the General Conference, G. A. Irwin and Harmon Lindsay.

The land was bought at the urging of Irwin. The property comprised a row of nine dilapidated slave cabins, a barn which leaned so heavily to one side that the men avoided going near it for fear it would collapse on them, and the plantation house, in desperate need of repair.

Towering high above them were many giant oak trees and because of those the location was given the name Oakwood Industrial School. The area in which the oak trees grew was to become the centre of the campus.

Once word circulated around the neighbourhood that a school was to be established on the land, two potential black students showed up and offered to help clean up the place. Olsen and Irwin were already doing the work in overalls.

An attempt to bring water to the site with buckets from a spring was not practical, so they set up a windmill over a well in a field, but two hours of pumping ran it dry.

Their third try for water was at an old well by the house. The two young men, along with a few others, were assigned to clear the well of seventeen feet of mud, knives, pitchforks, clevises, plough points, rock and other debris. The work went on for two days, and, when someone found a spur, one of the workmen told of a rumour that during the Civil War Confederates had dumped a Yankee cavalry man into the well.

The two young men were superstitious and lost no time in climbing out of the well. Work stopped, and no one could persuade them to continue digging. 'If that spur belonged to him,' they said, 'then the rest of him is still down there. And we aren't going to dig up the bones of a dead man.'

Work went on without them, and no bones were found. The well was finally cleared and fresh water again flowed on the plantation.

Another story about Oakwood College in its early days deserves to be told.

Agriculture was one of the main sources of income at the school, and as the latest methods in farming were used, many farmers in the area came to see how things were done. One farmer, however, resented a school for blacks. Unfortunately, in a fire, he lost everything: his barn, all his equipment, and even his animals.

On the day after the fire, Oakwood's farm manager loaded equipment and students and drove to the burned-out farm. Irritated, the farmer asked why they had come, and the manager replied they were there to harvest his crop for him.

The man was speechless. He had misjudged the Oakwood people, said he regretted doing so and asked for forgiveness. The manager replied that it had already been given.

During the noon lunch period, the farmer stopped the boys from eating their lunch and invited them inside his home instead for a dinner his wife had prepared. It was the first time he and his wife had eaten with black people. Prejudice had melted away.[17]

Oakwood College has grown to a size of nearly 1,300 acres. Many hope that in the near future it will be upgraded to university status. It has already started a graduate programme for a master's degree in Pastoral Studies.

An army of well-educated men and women, many of whom were students at Oakwood, now circle the globe proclaiming the Third Angel's Message and the soon return of Jesus.

Edson would be proud, and Anna Knight would no longer see black children learning to write by using sticks on the ground.

Thus, we come to the close of our word portrait on the second of the four boys who lived in the White house.

References

[1] Ellen G. White, *The Southern Work*, (Review and Herald Publishing Association).

[2] *Spirit of Prophecy Emphasis Week for Seventh-day Adventist Schools*, (Ellen G. White Estate, General Conference of SDA), 1974, page 32.

[3] Ronald D. Graybill, *Mission To Black America*, (Pacific Press Publishing Association), pages 19-20.

[4] *The Seventh-day Adventist Encyclopaedia*, Volume 10, (Review and Herald Publishing Association), page 1418.

[5] *The Gospel Herald*, Yazoo City, Mississippi, May 1898.

[6] *Spirit of Prophecy Emphasis Week for Seventh-day Adventist Schools*, (Ellen G. White Estate, General Conference of SDA), September 1968, page 29.

[7] Ronald D. Graybill, *Mission To Black America*, (Pacific Press Publishing Association), page 100.

[8] *Spirit of Prophecy Emphasis Week for Seventh-day Adventist Schools*, (Ellen G. White Estate, General Conference of SDA), September 1968, page 31.

[9] Ronald D. Graybill, *Mission To Black America*, (Pacific Press Publishing Association), page 116.

[10-13] *Ibid*, page 96.

[14] *The Gospel Herald*, Yazoo City, Mississippi, May 1898, page 1.

[15] *Ibid*, page 2.

[16] The story of Anna Knight is from *The Seventh-day Adventist Encyclopaedia*, Vol. 10, (Review and Herald Publishing Association), pages 873-4.

[17] The Oakwood College information came from two sources:-
Arthur W. Spalding, *Origin and History of Seventh-day Adventists*, Volume 2,

James Edson
Riverboat Evangelist

(Review and Herald Publishing Association), pages 349-352; and
Adventist World, February 2007, (Review and Herald Publishing Association),
pages 28-31. Article title, *The Oakwood Experience, Then and Now,* by
Michele Solomon.

The following reference was also used for details only; *Spirit of Prophecy
Emphasis Week for Seventh-day Adventist Schools,* September 1968, (Ellen G.
White Estate, General Conference of SDA), pages 27-32.

William Clarence
'Wilful Willie'

5

William Clarence White, nicknamed 'Willie', James and Ellen's third son, was born on 19 August 1854. Willie was curious, thoughtful and very sociable, but was, at times, difficult to manage.

There were times when Willie thought he was the only boy in the house, but his older brothers made it their business to remind him that they were there also. Although the youngest, Willie had ways of making his presence felt.

An example of this happened one night when the Whites were entertaining guests and Willie was put to bed early. His father firmly told him to stay in bed and go to sleep. James and Ellen White were both well aware that their son had a mind of his own; so 'Stay in bed!' was an order.

Sure enough, and true to form, Willie had plans of his own and they didn't involve staying in bed.

William Clarence
'Wilful Willie'

As the evening progressed, someone in the living room suggested they should sing, and Henry was asked to play the melodeon.

Meanwhile, Willie was wide-awake in bed. He was not about to go to sleep as he lay in bed listening. Shortly afterwards, his small figure, dressed in nightclothes, came out of the bedroom and he was singing at the top of his voice.

There were smiles from the visitors who thought it was cute.

Father, however, was not of that opinion. He picked Willie up, carried him back to the bedroom and put him to bed with firm instructions to stay there and go to sleep.

The singing began again. Willie himself tells what happened next.

'I jumped out of bed, in my nightgown, marched out into the large room and among the visitors. Father picked me up and put me back to bed.'[1] That time his father told him even more firmly to stay in bed and to go to sleep.

No one smiled or thought it was cute when it happened the third time.

Willie continues. 'Father picked me up and took me out through the kitchen to the back porch. There he laid me across his knee and administered a hearty spanking.'[1]

Willie never forgot that night, because years later as he recounted that story, he said, 'I remember today just how everything looked [as he was being spanked], especially the position of the moon as it hung over the boys' workshop. I thought seriously of my evil deeds, and resolved to be good.'[1]

But that was not the end of Willie's adventures. When he was about three years of age, his parents were building a house on Wood Street in Battle Creek. Money was scarce, but neighbours came to the rescue and practically built the entire place for them. Willie was excited as something new was happening every day he went there. He was especially thrilled when wallpaper was being hung.

At that time, Jenny Frazier took care of Willie while his mother and father worked. She began working for the family when they lived in Rochester, New York. The Review and Herald was located in that city and all employees lived with the Whites. It was a boarding house for fifteen people, and Jenny was hired to cook meals for all of them. And because money was hard to come by, turnips were substituted for potatoes. Uriah Smith, aged 22, one of the young boarders, said he didn't mind eating beans 365 days a year!

When the Review and Herald moved to Michigan, Jenny went along to work in the Whites' home.

One day, while Jenny was walking to the new house with Willie, she said to him, 'I don't want you to touch the paper on the walls.'

'Why?'

'Things are so dry, and dust is everywhere.'

'I'm not dusty.'

'Your hands might be, and the wallpaper is not dry yet. You could stain it or even stretch it in places if you touch it. We don't want it to wrinkle.'

Willie promised not to touch the wallpaper.

'Is that a real promise?'

'Yes.'[2]

When Willie saw the paper, he was itching to touch it. He wanted to feel it because there were flowers on it that looked real and he just *had* to find out if they were.

Jenny looked at him, knowing what he was thinking. But he had *promised.* As Willie ran from room to room, Jenny was right behind him.

Two neighbours came to see the house while they were there, and as Jenny talked with them, Willie flew past on his way to the kitchen.

'Careful!' called Jenny.

'I am,'[2] came the answer.

Once in the kitchen, Willie came face to face with the wallpaper. *'One touch won't hurt,'* he thought.

Slowly, very slowly, he reached out with one small finger. It felt so smooth, even the flowers. Next there were five fingers on the wall, then ten. Then he was running with both hands on the new paper. He was having a great time, and Jenny wasn't there to see him.

Jenny heard him and ran to the kitchen. It was empty, but there were screams. Then she and the other women saw a hole in the wall. Workmen had papered over a doorway that led to the basement, intending to cut the opening out later. But now they didn't have to as Willie had found it and had fallen through to the basement where he lay screaming.

Jenny ran to the basement and picked up the terrified boy. She felt for broken bones, but there were none, only cuts and bruises.

Crying and shaken, Willie was taken home. There was no spanking that time as it was felt that he had suffered enough punishment.

But he did manage to say, 'My hands were clean. I looked.'[2]

Did he learn his lesson? Let's find out.

Water was a problem. James White had large vats placed near the house so that when it rained water would fall from the roof and fill them. Yet, that was still not enough for cleaning and washing, so he had a large hole or cistern dug in the garden in which water from the roof could be stored for future use.

Willie was fascinated as that great hole was being dug. He watched it get deeper and deeper. Soon the workmen digging it could not be seen, but dirt kept flying out of the hole as they kept digging.

Thinking it was great fun to watch, Willie pulled his small rocking chair close to the hole to watch as dirt flew high into the air from people he could not see. So he rocked and watched.

In time, the men stopped for a lunch break and they climbed out of the hole.

No one noticed Willie's chair rocking closer and closer to the hole until they heard him scream. Willie and the chair had disappeared into the hole.

James White heard the screams, raced to the hole, placed a board across and swung down to the screaming Willie. People came running out of the house. He was taken out of the hole and examined, and since no bones were broken, everyone relaxed. There was no spanking that time either, as the terrified Willie had suffered enough.

William Clarence
'Wilful Willie'

Willie loved sitting on his mother's lap. One day he climbed up and sat contentedly – well, *almost* contentedly. Mother was reading and he didn't like that. He wanted attention and so deliberately put his head between her and the book she was reading. She gently pushed his head away. He did it a second time and she pushed his head a little harder. The third time he did it, she slowly put her book down, picked Willie up, turned him over, and gave him a good spanking. He never tried that trick again.[3]

My favourite story about Willie involves two other boys. Food was a problem in the early days of Adventist camp meetings. They had no refrigeration, supermarkets, or fast food places on hand. All canned food usually came from home canning, so, in order to have food at camp meeting, it had to be prepared ahead of time and brought from home. That was no easy job.

One hot day in Battle Creek, Michigan, three women were in a kitchen preparing food for a camp meeting, and one of them was Ellen White.

A boy named Herbert walked into the room and asked his mother, who was sitting there, if he could go across the street and play with Jimmy Root. Herbert's mother looked at Mrs Root, the third woman in the room, and asked if it would be all right for them to do that.

'Yes,' answered Mrs. Root. 'But, only if the boys stay on the porch and don't bother the neighbours.'

Herbert agreed, but before he left he turned to Ellen White and asked if Willie could come, too.

Her answer was, 'Yes, if you do as Mrs Root asks.'

Four boys in the White House

'We will,' shouted the boys as they ran off for the porch across the street.

The women continued their work, but as time passed, one of them felt nervous. Were the boys being good? Were they where they were supposed to be? She knew that not all children keep their promises.

Laying her work aside, she left the kitchen to check on the boys. She entered the parlour, crossed the room to a large window, and pulled back the curtain. She looked across to the Roots' house and saw that the boys were where they were supposed to be, but what she saw shocked her. Dropping the curtain she ran back to the kitchen to tell what she had seen.

The other women dropped what they were doing, and all three raced for the back door of the kitchen and were soon outside.

In those days women wore long, heavy dresses that touched, or almost touched, the floor. Throwing caution aside, the three pulled up their skirts, revealing their ankles, and ran. The boys saw them coming and took off down the street at speed. They knew what they had done, and that they were in trouble.

It had been a very hot day, and all three boys had taken off all their clothes!

There was no television or radio in those days, and much of the entertainment came from watching neighbours and their activities. There was plenty to watch that day as three grown women, with skirts held high, ran down the centre of the street chasing three naked boys!

And Ellen White was one of them.

The boys were caught, herded back to the house and into the kitchen. Everyone was out of breath. As they began to recover, Ellen White noticed the two women whispering and looking at her and, finally, one of them shyly asked if she would spank their boys for them. She didn't know how to answer until the woman continued. 'We think,' she said, 'it would make more of an impression on them if you did it.'

What did she do?

The answer is found in an old issue of *The Youth's Instructor.* This was a weekly paper published by the Adventist denomination for the youth of the church. James White had launched it as a monthly publication in August 1852 and the first issues were eight pages long.

Euphemia Wilson Parrish wrote the article that appeared in *The Youth's Instructor,* and in telling the story, she added that, 'he [Herbert] thought that he and Jimmy Root were the only boys in the [entire] denomination besides her own [Ellen White's son Willie] who had been spanked by the inspired messenger of the Lord.'[4]

Henry, Edson and Willie loved receiving letters and packages from their mother and father as they travelled. In one letter to Willie, Ellen White wrote, 'In the last box we sent to Battle Creek were some little trinkets for you and a little box of candy. You must eat it only when Jenny thinks it best. Eat a very little at a time. We hope you are a good boy.'[5]

Ellen White's travels often took her far from her children, but she never forgot them. In one letter to

Four boys in the White House

Willie she said, 'Dear Son Willie . . . bathe every week, twice a week if you can. You must go down to the house.' [Evidently he was staying with someone near their home]. Her letter continued, '. . . build a fire in the kitchen stove, and bathe. Rub yourself dry, . . . don't bother grandmother.'[6]

For all his bold childhood adventures, sometimes lucky, sometimes not, one feature stood out: Willie's thoughtfulness of others.

This is illustrated in an incident in 1863. Willie was nine years old, and the very first General Conference session was in progress. The meetings were held in Battle Creek, and because the weather was uncommonly hot and humid delegates were suffering. Realising that, Willie, on his own initiative, rushed home to find a pail and a tin dipper. After filling the pail with cold water, he walked up and down the aisles offering cool drinks of water to those hot, thirsty people. Serving others was one of his most marked and distinguishing characteristics for the rest of his life.

As he grew, Willie spent much of his time in or around the Review and Herald Publishing House. In 1935 he wrote to Grace Amadon, wife of a book trimmer, recalling earlier days when he worked with her husband at the Review and Herald. This is what he wrote.

'I used to count the pamphlets in bunches of five or ten and place them on a table, handy for him to reach and put into the machine. At the close of the day's work he would sometimes thank me, sometimes give me a few pennies and once in a while he would give me 15 or 20 cents after I had worked with him for two or three days.'[7]

His first real job, at the age of twenty, was in Oakland, California, for the *Signs of the Times.* That was before Edson began working there. Willie's job (for which his pay was less than a dollar a day) was to take, by wheelbarrow, type forms, printed sheets, and the published product to the printers and several other places of business, which were several blocks away.

While in California, Willie fell in love with a girl named Mary Kelsey, an assistant in the editorial area. The year was 1875 and they married on 11 February 1876.

Mary began work at the Review and Herald when she was almost thirteen years old and was baptised into the church soon afterwards. She advanced quickly in her job from the folding department to the type room and from there she was promoted to being a proof reader. Mary was also attending school at that time. At seventeen she went west to California to work for the *Signs of the Times* where she met Willie.

In time the couple returned to Battle Creek where Mary became one of the editors of *The Youth's Instructor.* They also enrolled in Battle Creek College for studies in French and German in order to prepare themselves to join J. N. Andrews in Europe to aid in his missionary work, but the trip never materialised. They did travel to Europe later, however, but under different circumstances.

In the meantime, Willie, because of a lack of leadership in the General Conference and his ability in administrative skills, was placed in several key denominational positions, some of which were to his liking while others were not. He also became highly involved in the newly organised Sabbath School Department.

In 1885, Grover Cleveland became the twenty-second president of the United States, the first Democrat to hold that office in twenty-five years. On 21 February the Washington Monument was dedicated. Then on 3 March the U. S. Post Office began special delivery service for first-class mail and 19 June saw the Statue of Liberty, a gift from France, arrive in New York City.

In August of that same year Ellen White sailed for Europe, accompanied by Willie, Mary and their two daughters. They were gone for two years.

Mary died in 1890. In 1891 Willie and his mother went to Australia, and it was there he met and married Ethel Lacey from Tasmania in 1900. Four sons and one daughter came from that marriage.

Although Willie was deeply involved in the offices and workings of the General Conference, his main efforts were devoted to assisting his mother in her travels and in publishing her writings. That resulted in the creation of the Ellen G. White Estate, now located in Washington, D.C.

Willie loved his mother, and there are scores of stories that could be told about that part of his adult life. Here is one which speaks volumes about his care for and devotion to his mother.

In 1893, Willie was 37 years old, and because his father had died, he took it upon himself to care for his mother. He did a good job.

During a camp meeting in New Zealand, his mother was sick. No one was to bother her as she needed peace and quiet to recover. But early one morning, she felt strong enough to go to the meetings. She knew if she told her friends, they would insist on her staying right where she was, but the more she lay in bed, the more her mind went to the meetings. 'They aren't far away,' she thought. 'They are only a mile down the road.'

Then she formed a plan of escape. She knew she could make it to the campground if she walked slowly and rested often. 'After all,' she reasoned, 'I am feeling better.'

The early-morning meeting was scheduled for 5.30am and to that one she determined to go. Slowly and quietly she got out of bed, dressed and left the house.

'Good,' she smiled to herself, 'everyone is still asleep, and no one saw me.'

But before she started for the road, she thought of the barn where there was a horse and buggy. Then she said to herself, 'That might be a better plan. If I can use them I won't have to walk.' Entering the barn, she found a two-wheeled cart and the horse in its stall.

'So far so good,' she smiled to herself.

But then she ran into a problem. The harness for the horse was located too high on the wall for her to reach. Then what? Well, she went back to her first plan. 'I'll walk,' she told the horse. 'You stay there.' So off she started.

She took small steps and walked slowly, stopping every so often to catch her breath as she was still very weak.

Yet nothing stopped her and she just kept right on going.

All of a sudden she heard a noise behind her and turned around but could see nothing because of thick fog. Yet the noise was getting closer. What was it?

Then she saw something emerging from the fog and heading towards her.

Her mouth fell open as she gasped, 'I don't believe it!' It was the cart she had seen in the barn, but there was no horse pulling it. She began to laugh. She just could not believe what she was looking at. Willie, her son, was pulling that cart. And he was shouting, 'Mother! Wait! Mother, wait!' What else could she do but wait?

As Willie pulled up beside her, he was puffing hard, wheezing and gasping to catch his breath. Finally, between gasps, he began to speak slowly. 'Mother, please get in the cart. You shouldn't be out here like this.'

'Willie!' laughed his mother, 'whatever are you doing? I can't get in that cart and let you pull it. I am too heavy for you to do it by yourself.' Still trying not to laugh, she added, 'What will people think when they see you acting like a horse?' Willie just motioned for her to get in and she climbed aboard.

Then it was Willie's turn to laugh. 'People will think,' he said, 'that I am just an old workhorse.' Then he added, 'I didn't have time to hitch up the horse when I saw you start out.' As the cart began to roll, Willie called out, 'Hold tight, Mother. We are on our way to camp meeting!'

People saw them coming as they neared the camp. Willie was huffing and puffing as he came down the road. A man named Star rushed to the rescue, and together they pulled the cart to the entrance of the main tent.

People did laugh when they saw what was happening. They had never seen horses like those before!

Willie didn't stay for the meeting. He went back to the house, then returned for his mother with a real horse to pull the cart.[8]

On the day of his death, 1 September 1937, Willie was working at the Ellen G. White Estate, which was located at Elmshaven, California, at the time.

In announcing his passing, the *Review and Herald* magazine, in its 16 September issue, made this comment. 'If those to whom he has done some kind deed or spoken some cheering word could bring a flower to his tomb, he would sleep beneath a wilderness of flowers.'

On the gravestone of Ellen and James White these words of Daniel 12:3 are engraved: 'They that be wise shall shine as the brightness of the firmament; and they that turn many to righteousness as the stars forever and ever.'[9]

William Clarence White rests beside his parents in the family plot in the Oak Hill Cemetery, Battle Creek, Michigan, where he awaits the appearing of his beloved Lord and Master to take him home after a job well done.

References

[1] *Spirit of Prophecy Emphasis Week for Seventh-day Adventist Schools,* Ellen G. White – The Human Interest Story, (Ellen G. White Estate, General Conference of SDA, 1972), pages 26-27.

[2] *Spirit of Prophecy Emphasis Stories,* Volume Four, (Ellen G. White Estate and the General Conference Department of Education, 1985), page 25.

[3] *Ibid,* pages 26-27.

[4] This story is based on *The Little Blue Chest, Part Two,* by Euphemia Wilson Parrish, and appeared in *The Youth's Instructor,* June 17, 1952. (Review And Herald Publishing Association).

[5] *Spirit of Prophecy Emphasis Stories,* Volume Two, (Ellen G. White Estate and the General Conference Department of Education, 1980), page 16.

[6] Letter in the White Estate marked W-9-1867, Johnstown, Wisconsin, September 19, 1867.

[7] *Spirit of Prophecy Emphasis Week for Seventh-day Adventist Schools,* Ellen G. White – The Human Interest Story, (Ellen G. White Estate, General Conference of SDA, 1972), page 27.

[8] *Spirit of Prophecy Emphasis Stories,* Volume Four, (Ellen G. White Estate and the General Conference Department of Education, 1985), pages 26-27. (The story was based on this reference.)

[9] *The Advent Review and Sabbath Herald,* Volume 114, number 42, October 21, 1937, page 17.

Also used for reference only was *The Bicentennial Almanac,* (Thomas Nelson Inc.).

Closing thoughts

The four boys who lived in the White house are long gone, but their memory endures. Henry, James Edson, Willie and John Herbert all lived, laughed, cried, and loved as children do.

Although God had chosen Ellen White for a special work on Earth, she also had a role as the mother of four boys. There were times, however, when she felt she had five boys for sometimes her husband behaved like a boy. She had her hands full!

Let us pause for a moment to consider some long overlooked information found in a series of books on Ellen White, written by her grandson, Arthur. The relevant section is a lengthy passage on pages 355 and 356 of volume number six in *The Later Elmshaven Years.*

Referring to manuscript 56a, written in the year 1911, Arthur White wrote, 'The document she has left us seems to be more of a "memorandum" than a testimony.'[1]

The contents of this 'memorandum' were given to Ellen White long before 1911, after her husband died, and this could be the reason for describing it as a memorandum.

It contains the following:

'I will appoint both your children that they shall strengthen your hands in sound judgement. But your youngest son shall carry the work with you . . .

'I will be his wisdom, I will be his judgement, and he shall work out in connection with his mother the important matters to come before the people.

'Both will be your helpers, in perfect agreement in conducting different lines of missionary work, standing firmly, unitedly, for great battles are to be fought.

'Your sons are of different temperaments. Your youngest will be your dependence, but the eldest shall be my minister to open the Word to very many people and to organise the work in various lines.

'Temptations will come to the eldest that preference in judgement shall be given to him above the youngest. But this cannot be. Both are to be guided by the light given their mother, and stand in perfect harmony.

'Let no jealousy come in because of the position I have appointed the youngest. I have put my Spirit upon him, and if the eldest will respect the position given the youngest, both shall become strong to build up the work in different lines. The eldest must be standing as ready to be counselled by the youngest, for I have made him my counsellor. There is to be no contention, no strife, no division, because I have given him from his birth special traits of character which the eldest has not.'

The Lord said, 'I will prove them both, but both must stand distinct and separate from influences which will be brought to bear to break up the plans I have marked out. But the youngest is fitted for a work that will make him counsellor, receiving the words from his mother. Both must carefully consider matters that I shall give.'

Ellen White was then given the following instruction:

'These things are not to be revealed to either until I shall instruct you, for both are to be proved. The time will come when you may have to speak all that I shall give you. . . . There will be a determination on the part of Satan to disarrange and break up my plan. A constant, ever-increasing confidence in the Word of God, and in the light given my servant, will keep these two workers blended; but the younger must be counsellor, when needed, to the elder.'

The document continues, 'Now you are at this period to open this matter to your sons. The instruction given, if obeyed, will be able to place things on the right bearing.'

The next sentence is heart-warming as this faithful little witness for God was told, 'You as a mother have suffered much, but you have not failed nor been discouraged.'

In the final passage we can only guess that relief came to Ellen White, leaving a feeling of warmth and comfort in her heart.

Four boys in the White House

It says, 'The eldest son has been sorely tempted and if he had closed his ears and heart to unwise counsellors, he would have stood a strong man. Now after he knows my purpose, the eldest must be transformed and the youngest must stand in the counsel of the Lord. He has borne his test wisely, and the Lord will help him to continue the work appointed.'[1]

Arthur White's comments on this passage were, 'The instruction moulded Ellen White's attitude towards her sons and when revealed was an encouragement to W. C. White. It would continue to be so in the days that followed, some of them difficult days. As questions were raised on inspiration, some of them sparked by the work done on the 1911 edition of *The Great Controversy,* W. C. White could stand in strength in his positions and attitudes moulded by closeness to his mother's work and subject to the influence of the Spirit of God. The effect on Edson was less noticeable. He continued to the close of his life to make a contribution to the cause of God, the last of which was in the production of evangelistic visual materials.'[2]

There is evidence of how this influenced Willie. One example is in a copy of the *Review and Herald* magazine dated 7 February 1907. Ellen White was the author and at the close of the article she recalled the time just after her husband died. She wrote as follows.

'For about a year after my husband died, I suffered greatly from sorrow. At that time, when I seemed to be hovering between life and death, my son Willie persuaded me to go a short distance in a phaeton [a light four-wheeled carriage] to a camp-meeting in Healdsburg.'

Note that it was Willie who persuaded his mother to continue her work, in keeping with what the Lord planned he should do. He was to provide help and be a guide for his mother and there he was doing just that.

Let's discover what happened as a result of Willie's urging his mother to attend that camp-meeting.

'A sofa had been placed on the platform in the large tent. Here I lay down, thinking I would deliver my farewell address. My face was as the face of one dead, without a particle of colour. . . . After a few testimonies had been borne, I asked Willie to help me to arise to my feet, and let me lean on him.' (Here again we note Willie's role in aiding and helping his mother.)

'There I stood, and began to tell the people that this was probably the last time they would ever hear my voice in camp-meeting. But after speaking a few words, I felt the Spirit and power of God thrilling through every nerve of my body. Those who saw me said that the blood could be seen as it put colour in my lips and reached my forehead. My flesh took on its natural appearance.'

What about those who were watching and listening to her? Were they affected by what they saw?

'One of the citizens of Healdsburg, in great surprise, turned to one of his neighbours and exclaimed, "A miracle is being wrought in sight of this whole congregation!"'

Four boys in the White House

And what was Ellen White's reaction?

'I could not understand why all were looking so intently at me, some even rising to their feet. The Spirit of the Lord had rested upon me, and I had been healed in the presence of a large congregation.' And the result? 'During the remainder of the camp-meeting, I spoke several times.'[3]

Fortunately, the White family still lives on through the lives they touched and the institutions they founded. It was not an easy road; hardships, disappointments, discipline and misunderstandings were part of their everyday life. Yet, there were fun times, too, such as when the boys toured the sights of old Boston, when they received letters from their mother, when they enjoyed music, or raised chickens and an occasional cow. Those were normal boys growing up in an unusual home, but it was one that was filled with love.

It was trips without the boys that were hardest on the family. The journeys James and Ellen White undertook were not joyrides, nor vacation excursions, but were fraught with hazards. The thought of leaving her children in the care of others bothered Ellen White most of all, and she wrote frequent letters home.

'Dear Children,' she began in one such letter, 'Henry, Edson, and Willie; I am as well as could be expected with all the travelling and broken rest. We left Newport Thursday morning. Rode three miles in a lumber wagon to Newport Village. Then took the stage [stagecoach] for Claremont – 14 miles. Took dinner at the hotel, the stage again for the depot, four miles farther, then the cars [railroad], and rode until eight o'clock at night, when we stepped out at St Albans, Vermont. Stopped at the hotel overnight.

'Took breakfast and then took our seats in the stage for Enosburg – 20 miles. I think it was. The horses were quite slow in ascending the hills. The stage carried us to Enosburg Falls, four miles from Brother Bourdeau's. We could not obtain conveyance to take us to the place of meeting. We waited for hours. After a long time we found a man with one horse and an old sheep rack, who took us to the place of meeting. The horse was poor and could not go much more than a walk. Your father had to walk up most of the hills, and the steepest pitches we both walked. We arrived at our destination at last, near the commencement of the Sabbath, all worn out, having eaten nothing but one cracker since morning.

'In the afternoon I had so much to write that we were late when we came into the entry of the meetinghouse. They told us we could not get in, for the house was crammed full. They sent us round to the back doors of the meetinghouse – a door each side of the pulpit designed to air the house, or rather relieve the speaker easily when the air was oppressive. By considerable crowding, gaining and pushing, we found our way into the house. People were sitting on the platform around the desk [pulpit]. On steps, and everywhere they could find a place, as thick as they could crowd together. The large gallery was full.

'While Brother Andrews was preaching I took paper and laid it on my Bible and finished the matter to be read to that large conference of delegates. I wrote five pages. Brother Andrews closed [finished speaking]. While they sang a hymn I put up pencil and paper, and when they had ceased singing I was upon my feet to talk.'[4]

In another letter from Lodi, Wisconsin, dated 5 March 1862, she wrote: 'Dear friends at home; . . . The babies [at the meeting place] made so much music [noise] and the houses were so small and we were crowded in so thick that it was wearisome to the nerves, and I have not obtained much rest in this place, although we were well used here and they do all in their power to make us happy.

'. . . Monday the snow was so drifted the brethren could not get home. We held a meeting in the schoolhouse Monday. Tuesday all started for home. Some lived 10 miles, some 16, 25, 30, 40, 50 and 60 miles away. They waded through the drifts three miles and returned. It was utterly impossible to proceed. Some have ventured out today, hoping to plough through the drifts. We start tomorrow to our appointment. We do not know if we can get through.

'James and self rode in a sleigh to Judah to take the cars. It was very cold. The air was piercing, but our buffalo robes did us good service.'[5]

They made it through to the train and left for Madison, arriving at four in the afternoon.

'We found two brethren waiting for us,' she wrote, 'to take us to Lodi. They had been waiting [since] 7.00 am. We decided to ride 20 miles that night. We asked the price of meals in the saloon [the saloon was usually a place for dining in most cities] and found the price fifty cents apiece. We ate a piece of cold bread and an apple, bundled up warm, and packed down on the bottom of the sleigh and rode until half-past one o'clock. Then stopped at Brother Chase's door, aroused them, and found the house was filled. One after another appeared until they numbered five, besides their own family. At two o'clock am we were shown to our bed and rested until morning.'[6]

Is it any wonder why they left their children in the care of others as they travelled?

Satan tried to do his work on that household. He wanted to destroy the Church and Ellen White by attacking her children. Henry knew that as he lay dying and pleaded with his brothers to live for God. Willie almost drowned, and Edson pounded the air at an unseen force as told by Ellen White in her book *Life Sketches*, page 138. But God, through prayer, came to the rescue, and both Edson and Willie survived.

While two of James and Ellen White's boys grew to adulthood, only one, Willie, had children. Strangely enough, he was the father of four boys, but there were also three girls.

References

[1] Arthur L. White, *Ellen G. White, The Later Elmshaven Years, 1905-1915*, (Review and Herald Publishing Association), page 355.

[2] *Ibid*, pages 356-357.

[3] *The Review and Herald Magazine*, 7 February, 1907, page 8. Also found in *The Spirit of Prophecy Emphasis Stories Volume IV*, (Ellen G. White Estate and the General Conference Department of Education) 1985, pages 24-25.

[4] Letter in the White Estate marked W-7-1863, Adams Centre, New York, 5 November, 1863.

[5] Letter in the White Estate marked W-4-1862, Lodi, Wis., 5 March, 1862.

[6] *Ibid*.

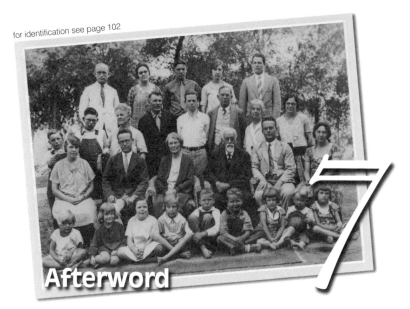

Afterword

7

I was fortunate enough to have known two of Willie's boys and one of his girls, Francis ('Frankie' as we called him), Arthur and Grace.

I became acquainted with Arthur because of my writing. He was in charge of the Ellen G. White Estate and was the person I had to deal with when I did research on his grandmother. He didn't know me, and I didn't know him, and there was strong tension and some resentment on his part towards me. We had several arguments, some of which I won, and some I didn't. However, over a period of time we became friends. Whenever he travelled west to California and to Pacific Press, where I worked, he would always visit my office. It was a delight for both of us.

Arthur was very protective of his grandmother's reputation and wrote volumes concerning her. His protectiveness was the reason that he was suspicious of me when I first began my research on her. Others had done that before and a few had distorted what they found and put Ellen White in a bad light. Satan even works among the files and papers of the White Estate. He knows what is there and, if he is allowed to have his way, he will twist and distort to his advantage what has been preserved in the estate's vaults. Arthur was determined not to allow that to happen.

Arthur was a scholar and a prolific writer, thorough and accurate in everything he did. His memory was phenomenal. Some say he ruled the estate with an iron hand, which may be true, but once I made a friend of him I found Arthur to be a warm, generous and delightful person. I liked him.

I used to ask him strange questions such as: 'Did Ellen White have false teeth?' He laughed, 'Yes, they both did.' Then he told of the time when they were staying with friends in Texas and the weather was bitter cold.

There was a twinkle in his eyes as he said, 'They had a habit of taking their teeth out at night and soaking them in a glass of water.' He went on to add that in the morning the lady of the house heard a strange sound coming from her kitchen. When she walked into the room, she found both James and Ellen White trying to chop their teeth out of solid chunks of ice with ice picks.

On one of my trips to the White Estate in Washington D.C., I asked Arthur this question. 'What did the angel look like who came to visit Ellen White in her visions?'

Arthur, without hesitation, told me exactly what that angel looked like but I didn't believe him.

Four boys in the White House

The information he gave is not found in any of Ellen White's writings and I later learned that it had been handed down from her to her family by word of mouth only.

A year or two later, Arthur was back in my office in California and I sprang it on him once more and again without hesitation he gave me the same answer, almost word for word.

That time I believed him. I knew him better by then and his answer made sense. This is what he said.

The angel who came to Ellen White, sometimes walking into her room, sometimes waking her up, looked no different from anyone who could be seen anywhere on the street. He was tall, well proportioned, with fine features, dressed in the clothes of the day, and he was young.

The part I had questioned was the fact that he was dressed in contemporary clothes. In other words, he appeared in the style and dress of her time. There were no wings, no shining lights.

This was new to me, but the more I thought about it, the more I accepted it, as it sounded reasonable. There were visions when Ellen White *did* see bright objects and shining wings, but not all the time. The young man's appearance did not startle her, because he looked like an ordinary man. I tried to find references to that angel, but all I could locate was a few statements describing him as 'the young man'.[1]

One Wednesday evening, Don Mansell was conducting a prayer meeting in the Adventist church in Nampa, Idaho. Don had at one time worked with Arthur White at the White Estate. In the middle of his presentation Don paused, looked at me and asked me to describe to everyone present what the angel Gabriel looked like. I was surprised, but I answered, 'I have no idea what Gabriel looks like.'

'Yes, you do,' he said. 'Arthur White told you about the angel that visited Ellen White.' I wasn't sure what Don meant until he added, 'I am convinced that her angel was Gabriel.' I then told the group what Arthur had said.

It took me several days to sort this thing out in my mind. But the more I thought about it, the more sense it made. Gabriel is ageless and appears all through the Bible record to various prophets and people of old, so why not to Ellen White? After all, her messages, vital information and instruction were from God, so what agent from God is better qualified to convey these things than Gabriel himself?

There is, of course, no proof of that. It is only a theory based on speculation, not on fact, by Don and myself.

Only Heaven has the answer, but it is something to think about.

Arthur died on 12 January 1991 in Yountville, California, but the work he so tenaciously guarded is well preserved to this day. He did a good job.

Frankie was quite different from his brother Arthur. He and his wife had two children, Charlie and Elaine, whom I knew. Frankie and I worked together at Pacific Press for years, and the longer I knew him, the more I felt he was like his father, Willie. He was laid back and friendly and had a great smile. I liked him and I miss him.

Four boys in the White House

Francis Edward White was the youngest child of Willie and May White. I was completely taken off guard when I first met him. I was working as a graphic designer for Pacific Press, and he was dressed in overalls and was a worker in the press foundry. I didn't expect to find a grandson of Ellen White in that position, but there he was. In time I got to know him pretty well. He laughed a lot and was fun to know.

Frankie was physically strong, loved water sports, and if anyone mentioned the word 'camping', he was ready to go. His sense of humour was choice. Once when I asked him to tell me about his father, he laughingly answered, 'My father never knew I worked at Pacific Press. He died before I was employed.'

I knew by the twinkle in his eyes that there was more to the story than that. So I waited for him to say more.

'I remember the day when my dad brought me to the Press to get a job. When he told me what the pay was, I laughed at him. I was young then and knew all the answers.'

Then looking straight at me Frankie said, 'But I'm here now.'

Then his mood changed; he was serious and he began to talk as if I was not there. 'I came back!' he said. 'He was a good dad. He taught us children how to work. He lived what he preached, and preached what he lived. He was away from home much of the time attending meetings. We were always glad when he came back with little treats that he always surprised us with.'

Another time, Frankie told me his father wore a long black coat, and when he came home from one of his trips he would walk into the house with his arms held high in the air. That was a cue for the children to mob him and attack the coat, as in the deep pockets were gifts for every one of them.

In another conversation, Frankie said, 'He often fell asleep on the speaker's platform during church. He did it a lot.'

This reminded me of something I had read which also revealed some of Ellen White's sense of humour; she did see the funny side of things when they happened. She was preaching one day when she noticed her audience was not listening: they were smiling, but not at her. Some were even sniggering and she wondered what was going on. She stopped speaking, turned around, and saw her son Willie sitting among the ministers on the platform, sound asleep.

She didn't wake him up. Instead she smiled, leaned over the pulpit, and in a soft voice, so as not to wake him, said, 'When Willie was a baby, James and I travelled a great deal. We used to put him to sleep in a little basket right in front of the pulpit where we could watch him. There he slept peacefully during all our sermons. Apparently he has not yet gotten out of the habit!' She then continued with her sermon.[2]

Frankie's big smile erupted into a low chuckle after he told about his father sleeping in church. Then he added, 'They sometimes called my father "Weeping Willie". Many times, when my father got up to speak in a church service or on another occasion, he would begin to talk about the pioneers in the Advent movement. He knew most of them. And when he did this he began to cry. It happened every time. That is why people began calling him "Weeping Willie".'

At one point in a conversation with Frankie, I sensed he was far away in thought. Then speaking as if I was not even there, he softly said to himself, 'That's my Pop.' There was a world of deep affection in those three simple words.

I asked Frankie if he had ever seen his grandmother.

'When I was a baby at Elmshaven [Ellen White's home in California], the children of the family would carry me up the back steps into Grandmother's room.' There was a single flight of stairs leading from the kitchen up to Ellen White's writing room, with a door at both ends. The grandchildren were told never to bother Grandmother when she was writing, but they loved to be with her.

They waited in the yard behind the house many times with their eyes on the kitchen, and when they saw that no one was about they would make a run for the door at the bottom of the stairs and creep up as quietly as they could. Ellen White always knew when they were coming. They would open the door to her room just enough to look inside and there they would wait until she put her pen down and turned to face the door. Then they would burst into her room and race across the floor to be with her.
(This is what Frankie was referring to when he said they would carry him up the steps to Grandmother's room.)

Frankie had more to add about those visits.

'Sometimes she would hold me. At other times they would set me on her bed, and she would play with me. I was only fifteen months old when she died.' He also told me that the other children said he loved playing with the buttons on Grandma's dress.

There were times when we at the Press would call Frankie 'Apple Annie'. That happened in the autumn of the year when Frankie would pull a two-wheeled trailer behind his car into the Press car park. On the trailer were boxes of Gravenstein or Red and Yellow Delicious apples for sale. We depended on that, and he never disappointed us.

Frankie told me several delightful stories about his days at the Press and one in particular amused me.

He and a colleague were working late one night. It was very hot and they were tired, and in time Frankie had had enough. He laid his work down, looked at his friend and said, 'I'm going swimming.'

In those days Pacific Press had an indoor swimming pool.

'We can't do that,' came the answer. 'The rule is a lifeguard must be on duty whenever someone is swimming. There isn't one tonight. The pool is closed.'

'Lifeguard or not,' answered Frankie. 'It's too hot, and I'm going swimming.'

'If you go, I will too.'

They went to the pool, took off all their clothes and dived in. It was cool and pleasant; they were refreshed and were enjoying the swim.

Suddenly an outside door to the pool began to open. In stepped Arthur S. Maxwell who had late guests, a key, and wanted to show off the indoor pool. They came inside.

'What did you do?' I asked Frankie.

He laughed and said, 'I never took so many deep dives in all my life.'

Needless to say, Maxwell and company beat a hasty retreat.

Grace Jacques was another of Willie's children and I made friends with her while she was the official guide for Elmshaven. She enjoyed having her picture taken, so I took several. Grace had beautiful white hair, a gravelly voice, and like Frankie, laughed a lot. She told me many stories.

When I was visiting once, she pointed to a number of bees in Ellen White's writing room. 'They have been there for years,' she said. 'They are in the wall and we can't get rid of them. We live with them, and they live with us.'

She also pointed to a large pine tree in front of the house. 'I got married under that tree,' she said and it was near that tree that Grace told me the following story. She was laughing so much as she told it I almost missed what she was saying.

In 1900, when Ellen White left Australia to return to the United States, Willie and his family sailed with her. When the ship stopped at one of the islands in the South Pacific, many passengers wanted to go ashore. But the water was too shallow for the ship to dock. So native islanders came in small boats and took passengers aboard. But then the water became too shallow even for them. So, for the last part of the trip ashore, natives carried passengers to the beach in their arms.

When Ellen White's turn came, two natives formed a seat by joining hands. She sat on that makeshift seat, with her arms around their necks, and they sloshed ashore.

Once they reached dry land, the natives sat her on top of a large rock from where she enjoyed watching fellow passengers being carried in like manner. It was a sight to see!

One after another came. Then something made Ellen White laugh. At first, her laughter was quiet, but as she continued to watch it became stronger and louder. In time she was laughing so hard she began to rock back and forth until she slipped and fell off the rock. People came running to her rescue. She was unhurt, but still laughing.

This is what she had seen. Willie's wife, Ethel, usually referred to as May, her middle name, was being carried ashore by a large, strong native. All he had on was a brief cloth around his waist. Ethel was sitting on his back with a vice-like grip around his neck and he was having difficulty breathing. Her legs were wrapped around his waist, and her long dress was wadded up in her lap. In one hand she held an open umbrella and she was slipping and sliding across the man's slippery back. But that was not all: the man was holding, under one of his arms, Ethel's baby, and it was screaming. It was something to be seen as the exhausted native finally set Ethel and her baby on dry land.

When I took my parents on one of my trips to Elmshaven, Grace and my mother became instant friends. One of their conversations concerned their ailments, arthritis being the main topic. They talked on and on.

Just before we climbed into our car to leave, Grace came running from around the back of the house. She was dressed in her gardening clothes with worn-out shoes. She came as fast as she could, as she wanted to tell mother something she had forgotten.

'I think I have a cure for arthritis,' she said, trying to catch her breath.

Mother listened and took notes of what she said. I still don't know what she told her, but they were both quite serious about it. My father, who was not a Seventh-day Adventist, was also very impressed with Grace.

The last time I saw her was during a tent-meeting at Yountville, California. She was sitting quietly on the first row. Her hair was snow white. She wore a dark dress trimmed with a large white lace collar, and she looked beautiful.

Willie and his second wife, Ethel May, had twin boys, Henry and Herbert.

In 1897 the twins were just emerging from babyhood, and Ellen White was enjoying them immensely. Often, when the weather was cold, they were dressed alike in small red coats with white hats.

In a letter to Willie, who was in the United States, his mother wrote, 'The boys are hearty fellows. I think it will cost you something to feed them. They can take a few steps now, and are in good health. Today Herbert put his finger in Henry's mouth, and Henry bit it. Oh, how Herbert did cry! For some time he would not look at Henry without crying. But they seldom cry when they hurt themselves.'[3]

She also added that she and Sara, Ellen White's travelling companion and nurse, had taken the boys for a ride to pick up the Haskells. While they were doing that, the boys went to sleep. Henry woke up when they reached the town of Morriset, took one look at Elder Haskell, 'and his upper lip was thrown out until it was quite prominent. Then he looked at his grandmother, cuddled himself down, and went to sleep again, and slept until we arrived home.'[4]

Another time when horses and a wagon were ready to take Mrs White to the post office, the boys saw it, 'and both came running to their grandmother with their little arms outstretched, full of expectation that I would take them. I did not have the heart to disappoint them. Their wraps were thrown on and Sara cared for one and I for the other, and then they were perfectly happy, having a hold of the end of the lines and supposing that they were driving.'[5]

'Tuesday 10 May 1898. Sara and I rode out two miles to a lemon orchard. We obtained the native lemons for twopence a dozen – four cents in American money. The twins, . . . now 25 months old, were very much pleased, gathering the lemons and piling them up in heaps, and with their unintelligible language showing them to grandma.'[6]

The boys loved chattering to birds and even logging bullocks along the various roads.

Monday 27 June 1898 found them picking lemons again. They backed their wagon under the trees where Sara stood on it picking the fruit. 'The two-year-and-half-year-old twins enjoyed this very much, but their hands were not strong enough to pull the lemons from their firm fastening. Sara pulled the fruit for them.'[7]

In a letter to Emily Campbell in 1896, Willie wrote: 'I take care of the horse, May [his wife] looks after the chickens, and Mabel [another child] feeds the cats. Henry and Herbert [the twins] put in most of their time feeding themselves. They are growing finely, and begin to respond when you talk with them. Their vocabulary is not large, but they can say goo and gee and gaa, and when they are hungry they can yell loud enough to be heard to the police station.'[8]

One more thing should be added before leaving the baby twins. They were living at a time when a new school was being built in Australia, a school for future generations of young Seventh-day Adventist men and women. But what was it really like to live there in those early days? Were there dangers, especially for small children? A written record exists in the Ellen G. White Estate that was by Willie himself. In it he gives a brief picture of how primitive and wild it was. They were brave, hard-working people. The writing appeared in a paper known simply as the *Record* and the date was March 1898. The article concerns the animal life in the area, both domestic and wild, and reads as follows:

'Of domestic animals and other living creatures on the place, the school has three farm horses, about a dozen cows, half as many young cattle, and forty to fifty fowls. Besides this, there are twenty-two swarms of bees, from whose summer gatherings of honey eleven hundred pounds have already been extracted and stored for the winter use of the students.

'Of the wild animals on the place, we cannot speak so definitely. There is a small family of kangaroos, which show themselves occasionally. The wallabies are quite numerous, although many have recently been shot. Thus far they have not done serious injury to our crops. The native bears are getting scarce. We seldom hear their cry. Opossums can be heard any night, although they have been thinned out by the hunters. Snakes are much talked about, but rarely seen. Each year we see less and less of them. Occasionally a tiger cat makes a raid on our fowls. Then we trap him, and he suffers the death penalty for his 'fowl' murders. Flying foxes have done us no harm this year. Of magpies, there are plenty. The laughing jackasses, though not numerous, are very sociable. Groups of cockatoos and parrots are occasionally seen. The bell bird and the whip bird can be heard every day.'

When the twins grew to manhood, they went into the printing business. As their business grew they saved enough money to buy a used car. It was a one-year-old model T Ford, a touring car. May wrote to Willie about it in a letter dated 6 July and stated that the twins boasted they could travel 100 miles on a dollar's worth of petrol. They loved that car and even persuaded their grandmother to ride with them. She wrote, 'I took my first ride in it. It is the easiest machine I have ever ridden in.'[9]

In a corner, on the third shelf of a wall cabinet in the Pacific Press museum, sits a large, full-colour picture. It is quite old and is a cover for a few sample pages from a book titled *Peking The Beautiful.* The publication date, as far as I can tell, is 1928, and it was printed in China. A white border surrounds the picture on the cover, and on that border is a handwritten message in ink. It is a Christmas greeting to H. G. Childs, president of Pacific Press, and his wife, from the author of the book, Herbert C. White.

Henry and Herbert had gone to China as missionaries to open and operate a publishing house for the Adventist Church.

On the inside pages of this copy are two references to the publishers. One lists Herbert as art director of the Signs of the Times Publishing House in Shanghai. The other publisher's reference is The Commercial Press Ltd., C 453 Honan Road, Shanghai, China, 1928. (It is my opinion that those two were one and the same.)

The original book was quite large, measuring roughly 12 inches wide by 16 inches tall. It is described as being printed on handmade, double-edged, buff-toned parchment and bound in silken tapestry, charmingly executed in six colours by the Nanking silk factories. The price in China was $60.00. In the United States it sold for $45.00 gold coin. It carries a formal introduction by Dr Hu Shih, a celebrated Chinese scholar, philosopher, and leader of the Chinese Renaissance.

A book review also appeared in a newspaper called the *China Journal.* At that time it was the foremost magazine on science and art and this is what it stated:

Afterword

'We can best give an idea of the photographs in this wonderful book by saying that each in itself is a work of art, a picture in the real sense of the word, while those who made them are true artists. Certainly the pictures convey as nothing has done heretofore an adequate idea of the beauties of the great Northern Capital.'

The book also carries words of appreciation from Princess Der Ling. 'While looking through this album, I feel as though I was once more at home within the encircling walls of old Peking. I appreciate especially the subdued, harmonious tones throughout; for they are coloured just as the Empress Dowager would have wished them. While I was with her at the Summer Palace I saw the pavilions being repainted, and the Empress always insisted on subdued effects in the colouring of palaces and pavilions.' *The Chinese Journal* reported that Henry, Herbert's twin, had also worked on the book.

Thus, Herbert and Henry (whose vocabulary once consisted of 'goos, gees and gaas', and who possessed such powerful lungs that when they opened their mouths and yelled, as their father Willie described, 'loud enough to be heard at the police station') grew up to impress the elite of China with their literary and artistic skills. Their influence even earned the admiration of a royal Princess of old China!

The period of living and pioneering in Australia, where the twins were born, was among Ellen White's happiest years. She felt completely at home on that continent.

Four boys in the White House

The influence that parents have on their children can last a lifetime and this was especially true for the children of James and Ellen White. Evidence of this can be found in one of the first issues of the *Signs of the Times,* written when James Edson was in charge of that publication. In volume one, dated 22 July 1875, he wrote an article on tobacco. It appeared in a section under the title 'Health Department' and its headline reads: 'Tobacco as a Medicine.' His mother had campaigned against the use of tobacco, and then he took up the cause. The first paragraph begins: 'We hold that tobacco is essentially bad, an unmitigated curse, as well to the health as to the pocket, of every consumer. Not only this, but it is almost impossible to conceive of a worse nuisance in society. In the crowded street, in the railroad car, on the steamboat, in the lecture hall, in the church, and in the parlour, the tobacco-user makes himself an object of disgust to everyone who does not defile himself by the use of the filthy weed.'

His article went on to point out that tobacco is of no good to anyone even though contemporary doctors were pointing to it as a cure for many ailments. He called it a powerful narcotic with damaging effects.

His strong antipathy towards the use of tobacco was first instilled when he was a boy, and it stuck. Here is a powerful argument of parents' influence on their children.

Ellen White was always thinking of other people. While living at Sunnyside in Cooranbong, Australia, her working staff became discouraged over some matter. As they arrived for work one morning, they discovered that Ellen White had been there before them. She had been thinking of them because, on a blackboard, in her own hand, were these words: 'Be pitiful and kind to each other. Everyone is fighting a hard battle.'[10]

Before closing our glimpse into the lives of the children of James and Ellen White, I should like to introduce you to a man I have never met, (I have neither seen nor talked with him and I don't even know what he looks like), but with whom I correspond. I now call him friend.

Earlier in this narrative we became acquainted with his mother, Grace Jacques. So now, through one of his letters, I present Oliver Jacques, a great-grandson of Ellen White, who lives with his wife Fredonia in Southern California.

He wrote one letter in particular that speaks in detail of the lasting influence on him of his grandfather, Willie. I here quote from that letter with Oliver's permission.

'Until I was seventeen, I had a close relationship with W. C. White. I worked with him in the garden, chopped wood with him, travelled with him on the trains, and did a lot of driving for him. You may know that he never learned to operate a car. On a camping vacation, he and I slept out under the stars. I still remember the smell of cheese grass.

'Grandpa was a great swimmer and taught us all how to swim. When he was eighty, our family and EGW staff went to Russian River for a day of fun. In our bathing suits, he and I approached the high dive.

Four boys in the White House

The highest springboard was 30 feet high. "I bet you can't dive off the top board," I challenged. Saying nothing, he climbed to the top platform and, without hesitation, dived into the water below. It was an interesting sight, the little old man with a beard, and in an ancient bathing suit, flying through the air.

'Grandpa loved and enjoyed his many grandchildren. In 1928, the year of the "Great White Reunion", all his children and grandchildren lived in his house for several months, some for years! We knew him well. He showed his affection. Always a "goodnight" kiss. Sometimes a "good morning" kiss. Lots of hugs. He could be firm. Disobedience was unthinkable.

'Dinner was always a treasured event. Grandma set a marvellous table. There were frequent guests. With eyes open, looking at the food, Grandpa would say the blessing. The plates were stacked at his place. With a word of appreciation to his 'English queen', (his nickname for his wife), he would fill her plate first. Always first! Then children and adults. Everyone waited for Grandma to lift her fork. If a grandchild misbehaved, there was a word of reproof from Grandpa, but mealtime was a happy occasion.

'When he had eaten, there was always a funny story. I can't imagine where he got them all! Many had a New England flavour! I once stayed six months with my grandparents. I seldom heard the same story twice!

'Particularly memorable were the Sabbath afternoon walks through the woods. Lots of stories, also, listening to tales of "early days" about "Mother and Father" and the "Brethren" while sitting on the front porch.

'Friday night worships will never be forgotten. Singing Advent hymns. A scripture read by Grandpa. (When he read a psalm or other passage, he lived the part. When David rejoiced or laughed, Grandpa did the same. When David cried, Grandpa cried.) My mother [Grace] said it was the same with Ellen. Hearing and reading of Scripture was a treat.

'I shall never forget the Sabbath evening worship two weeks before his death. After the hymns and scripture (Rev. 21:22) we all knelt for prayer. Customarily, everyone two or older prayed. As we arose, he slowly looked into the eyes of each one present. Then, quietly, but with an earnest tone, said, "Let's all be there." Stories by the fire followed by hugs and kisses. I was seventeen, but got my share. What a bonding! I felt the loss of his friendship for years after his death. My decision to study for the ministry was inspired by him. I wanted to be like Grandpa.'

Is it any wonder that the children of James and Ellen White, with the training and guidance given them, should become nothing less than kind, caring and thoughtful adults? Francis White's memories of his father and Oliver's letter prove that. The work those pioneers did for the Seventh-day Adventist Church continues to this today.

Four boys in the White house aren't there anymore, but what a life-story they gave us!

I hope to meet them someday.

How about you?

References

[1] E. G. White, *Counsels on Health,* Page 465, and *Life Sketches,* page 208, (Pacific Press).

[2] From an interview with Francis White, and a reference in *The Spirit of Prophecy Emphasis Stories,* vol. 4, (Ellen G. White Estate, and the General Conference of SDA), page 118.

[3] From a letter by Ellen White (in the White Estate) catalogued as letter 241, 1897.

[4] From a diary entry of Ellen White's dated 3 May 1897.

[5] From a manuscript in the White Estate, catalogued as MS 173, 1897.

[6] From a manuscript in the White Estate, catalogued as MS 182, 1898.

[7] From an Ellen White diary entry dated 27 June 1898.

[8] From a Willie White letter, located in the White Estate by Willie White to Emily Campbell, dated 3 August 1896.

[9] Part of a letter dated 6 July 1913 from May White to her husband Willie. The original is in the White Estate.

[10] *Spirit of Prophecy Emphasis Week for Seventh-day Adventist Schools,* (Ellen G. White Estate, and the General Conference of SDA), September 1969, page 56.

Photographic Identification Page 82

Back row: Dr John Jacques, Grace White-Jacques, Francis White, Frieda Swingle-White, Arthur L. White.

Second row standing: Wilfred Workman Jr, Clifford Workman, Mabel White-Workman, Wilfred D. Workman, Virgil Robinson, Dores E. Robinson, Ella White-Robinson and Mabel Robinson.

Third row seated: Anna Johnson-White, Herbert C. White, Mrs W. C. White, Elder W. C. White, J. Henry White and Margaret Rossiter-White.

Front row: Viola Jacques, Dorothy White, Gladys Robinson, Kathryn White, Oliver Jacques, Sylvan Jacques, Daphne White, Donald White and Winnifred White.

Notes